OLD WORLD
WISCONSIN

AROUND EUROPE IN THE
BADGER STATE

Fred L. Holmes

HEARTLAND PRESS
an imprint of NorthWord Press, Inc.

i

OLD WORLD WISCONSIN

AROUND EUROPE IN THE BADGER STATE

Fred L. Holmes

Copyright © 1944
Fred L. Holmes

Second Edition © 1990
Book designed by
Lakeland Graphic Design
Minocqua, Wisconsin

Cover designed by
Marathon Press, Inc.
Wausau, Wisconsin

NorthWord Press, Inc.
Box 1360
Minocqua, WI 54548

For a free catalog describing NorthWord's line of
nature books and gifts, call 1-800-336-5666.

ISBN 1-55971-056-X

Cover photograph by Jim Umhoefer

PREFACE

APPROXIMATELY 50 years ago, Fred Holmes was among those foresighted people who realized that Wisconsin's amazing cultural diversity should be recorded before many elements disappeared. The result was his classic volume, *Old World Wisconsin: Around Europe in the Badger State*. The book stimulated interest in Wisconsin's ethnic heritage and went through several printings. Libraries fortunate enough to own a copy of the 1944 work frequently keep it under close tabs in the reserved section.

A contemporary of Holmes, architect Richard W.E. Perrin, saw examples of Wisconsin's ethnic architecture in peril and argued for their preservation. Perrin's interest and awareness of Wisconsin's unique architectural heritage was piqued by his work with the Historic American Buildings Survey in the 1930s. A 1953 visit to outdoor museums in Germany and Scandinavia convinced him that something similar should be done in Wisconsin. As a result of Perrin's writings and repeated appeals over the next decade, the Board of Curators of the State Historical Society of Wisconsin was convinced of the need for a museum of ethnic architecture and approved the concept in 1964. After assessing several sites for the museum, a site was selected in the southern unit of the Kettle Moraine State Forest and named Old World Wisconsin.

Today, Old World Wisconsin is one of America's outstanding outdoor museums and the only one portraying the contributions of so many ethnic groups. Historic buildings from throughout Wisconsin are grouped into ten farm units depicting the heritage of immigrants from Germany, Poland, Norway, Denmark, and Finland as well as Yankees from the eastern United States. A crossroads village with a church, town hall, inn and several craft shops features the homes or shops of people from England, Ireland, and Bohemia. None of the over 50 buildings at Old World Wisconsin are reproductions or reconstructions. All were actually built by early settlers in Wisconsin and many clearly show the ethnic background of their builders.

Old World Wisconsin is more than a museum of ethnic architecture. Through authentically costumed interpreters in all major buildings, the daily lives of early Wisconsin immigrants are acted out. A visitor can see the Bohemian shoemaker at work, talk to a German farm wife baking bread, or enter the sauna as a Finnish family prepares for its twice-weekly ritual. Surrounding each farm and village residence are gardens producing each family's favorite vegetables, as well as field crops appropriate to the time period and ethnic background of the family. In the barnyards and meadows are farm animals and poultry of breeds well-known to the immigrants.

I believe Fred Holmes would enjoy Old World Wisconsin as it exists today and would be pleased to see how the museum is preserving the building styles and traditions he felt were slipping away back in the 1940s.

Hugh D. Gurney
Director
Old World Wisconsin

CONTENTS

CHAPTER I

Romantic Days Are Fading
Green Bay and Chippewa Falls

WOULD you like to see historic places, authentic relics, hallowed ground? Would you like to hear the French folksongs of the first settlers sung by present-day descendants? Would you like to walk in paths bordered by old-fashioned flower gardens? Green Bay has all of them.[1] She was the gateway to the Middle West opened wide by Frenchmen whose ineradicable imprint is still discernible after the passing of nearly two centuries.

A Frenchman's cottage is the oldest residence in Wisconsin. Jacob Roi, a voyageur, built it at La Baye in 1775. It is preserved in a public park as a memorial to the romantic days of the French traders and trappers by a city that has since Americanized itself as Green Bay.

Before the old house became the property in 1850 of Nils Otto Tank, a Norwegian nobleman of royal lineage, it had witnessed many strange and turbulent scenes. Whenever I visit Green Bay, I enter the ornamental door of the low-eaved dwelling to have Father Time escort me to a chair before one of its many paned windows in a room heavy with the scent of mellowed pine wood. Before that window once passed in succession the "tawny Sioux, wily Fox and fierce Winnebago, journeying eastward to help their British 'father' fight the 'long knives' along the Detroit frontier." Through that window Judge Jacques Porlier, who bought the old house in 1805, paused in his work to look out at his daughter, "la chere petite Marguerite," snipping flowers in their beautiful garden. Within these walls the legal business of La Baye hamlet was transacted — contracts for furs executed,

1

civil marriages solemnized and rumors of war debated. Through these windows, the flickering light of the candles told the passing wayfarer of gay social gatherings casting long shadows on dancing partners made momentarily joyous by the music of the French fiddler keeping time with his foot to:

> " 'Tis Money Musk by merrie feet
> And the Money Musk by heart."

Wisconsin is cognizant of its debt to the intrepid French explorer, priest and trader. Soon to stand in the shadow of the capitol dome at Madison will be the Bedore statue of Jean Nicolet, the first white man to come to Wisconsin, who arrived at the Green Bay entrance in 1634; in the streets of De Pere, a tablet marks the site of the first mission founded by Pere Claude Allouez in 1670;[2] the black-robed Father James Marquette, co-discoverer of the Mississippi in 1673, is one of two representatives of the state in Statuary Hall in Washington; Charles de Langlade, "the bravest of the brave," who created the first farm out of the wilderness, is memorialized by a bronze cenotaph in the city of Green Bay; "Villa Louis" at Prairie du Chien and the "Grignon House" at Kaukauna have been rehabilitated to perpetuate the high cultural attainments of the French; and two State parks — Perrot and Brunet Island — designate localities where French fur traders conducted extensive operations.

The early French who came to Wisconsin were pathfinders rather than empire builders. They preferred to trap — to wander in wilderness solitudes, and to puff a pipe at night around the fire, while telling other loiterers of the incidents and exploits of the day. Their observations on the cunning of wild animals — the ingenuity of the beaver, the wariness of the muskrat — interspersed tales of their own courage and fearlessness. The harsh struggle for existence and the rugged outdoor life gave these people an individuality of their own.

But war shattered the silence of their woodland security. The Black Hawk episode that made a trail across southwest Wisconsin in 1832 was to hasten the decline of the fur industry's supremacy. Soldiers scouting through the brush, around silver lakes, across verdant meadowlands and along fertile valley bottoms in search of the fleeing Sacs came to realize the possibilities for developing a home in such a country of contagious beauty and wild productivity. Their letters back home stirred the East. Soon came the New Englanders and New Yorkers — typical, farseeing Yankee stock, who were to run the governmental affairs of Wisconsin in pretty much their own way until the end of the century. The greatest advance in American history had begun to take form and was to roll westward until the vast continent was subjected to settlement.

Opportunity breeds epochs. The Old World heard the gossip of cheap lands and freedom here in the MiddleWest. English, Germans, Norwegians, Hollanders, Irish, Belgians, Swiss and people of other nationalities crowded the boats to reach this land of promise. Between June 1846 and December 1847, the population of Wisconsin increased by 55,000, a gain of about 30 percent. To expedite the tide of newcomers into the state an immigration department was created in 1852. Recurring waves of settlement continued to beat against our shores from every country in Europe until about 1915, finally to inundate much of the remaining unoccupied fertile acres. Meantime the state had become the most varied melting pot for both rural and urban foreign colonizations in the nation.

Seemingly each group caught the same vision — work, plant, build, and develop a better, freer Wisconsin. The trails of the explorer, the hunter and the settler now became the highways by which the state was to rank first in the market with its butter, cheese, peas, and other products. Gradually the French entrepreneur receded further into the shadows.

Green Bay and Prairie du Chien still radiate French tone and charm. Now and then a poet has caught from villagers strange snatches of song or a touch of romantic levity laden with memories from Normandy, Brittany, or Quebec:

SUNDAY [3]

For the Frenchman—1830
Pere Constant say
Sunday is big fete day
That mean for play
Just so we go to masse,
He don't care he
What we do then
So long we don't commit a mortal sin.
The venial ones, he say,
We goin' do anyway,
Then we confess to him.
The priest ain't goin' to have no job
If we don't sin a little bit.
And life, by gar,
The Irishman say by gory,
Ain't goin' to be some fun
If everybody in it
Is so damn good
That he can't smile
When Sunday come along.
By gosh, I think I prefer stay
With Irishman in purgatory.

For more than a century the French influence has been fading. Those who came as soldiers and traders in colonial times turned into farmers as economic conditions changed. Since 1800, few immigrants have arrived directly from France. Those who did come were French Canadians and their increasing numbers became so noticeable that the census now makes its report only under that designation. There are over 22,000 people of French extraction in the state, with 3,141 in Milwaukee County; 2,027 in Marinette County; 1,600 in St. Croix County; 1,362 in Chippewa County; and 1,148 in Brown County. Green Bay is still the center of French influence with 766 foreign and native-born scattered throughout the city. Other larger urban colonizations are at Bay Settlement, Cadott, Chippewa Falls, Coleman, Fond du Lac, Lena, Marinette, Martell, Niagara, Oconto, Paoli, Prairie du Chien, Rice Lake, Somerset, Superior, and Two Rivers.[4] Still other places now passed away have left memories behind.

Three epochs of history mark the settlement of the French in Wisconsin. Many of the first to arrive were traders and trappers who came directly from France to engage in the fur trade; the second influx came mostly from the French province of Quebec just before the Civil War and became active in the lumbering industry; the third were the remnants of both groups who remained to farm, once the timber had been removed and the log drives ended. This explains the presence of French settlements along the rivers of Northern Wisconsin.

With the opening of the Chippewa Valley for logging, the French Canadians arrived in such numbers that they became the founders of many villages within a radius of fifty miles around Chippewa Falls. Working in the woods as lumberjacks had always had a fascination for them. They are generally accredited as having been the best river men of the traditional and exciting Wisconsin log drive, now only a fond memory. Some there followed the lumbering industry to the Pacific Coast. So influential were they in the olden days that on the feast of St. John the Baptist, June 29, the saw mills closed in Chippewa Falls to permit them to attend church and march in processions. This feast day is still observed but not on such an elaborate scale.

In several Northern Wisconsin communities where other foreign groups settled as neighbors to the French Canadians, it was often necessary for the Catholic priest to read the gospel in three or four different languages at Sunday mass. The story was told to me of a pastor in Cadott who used to say, "Now, everybody sit down except the Irish" (and then read in English). "Now everyone sit down except the French"; and so on until each nationality had its turn. Not until World War I was this custom discontinued[5] and the reading in English alone decided.

Unlike their Old World cousins, the French Canadians were definitely prolific, the average family consisting of twelve individuals. As a result there are many people of French Canadian extraction living in Wisconsin with the same family name and surname. Among the more common family designations are: Bassette, Billard, Blanchard, Boucher, Baudreau, Brazeau, Carneilier, Cote, Duval, De Mars, Gagnen, Gaulet, Gingras, Grillot, Herbert, La Plante, La Valle, Le May, Loiselle, Parent, Peloquin, Peliter, Rivard, Sinette, Tradeau, Toutant, and Tremblay. Due to the fact that many of the early French settlers were illiterate, their descendants often spell and pronounce their names according to English diction — Renault has become Reno, Gagnon has become Gonyea, and Paquette has been changed to Poynette.

While visiting among the French, I think pea soup was served at meals more often than any other dish. It is accorded the place of a staple in their diet. Coffee is the customary drink. They like tourtieres (meat pie); maple syrup with pancakes; French-fried potatoes; fish, highly seasoned; salt pork and special pastries. If the priest calls on a Friday, a special meal with eggs is likely to be the principal dish on the table. The eggs are poached in maple syrup and served floating in the syrup — like a horizontal sunset in miniature. Besides Galette cookies, the dessert may consist of a pudding made by the stewing of dried pumpkin in syrup, served with a maple syrup sauce and topped with whipped cream.

"When spring comes and the sap begins to run, the French makers of maple syrup get awfully busy, all at once," explained Louis Blanchard, a typical French farmer who owns a twenty-acre sugar bush on the banks of the Chippewa River near Cornell. Several other bushes are operated by French in Marinette County.

"The harvest lasts only a short time," continued Mr. Blanchard, who has "syruped" for more than forty years. "Supplies to last our people a year must be prepared in a few days. Since it takes thirty gallons of sap to make a gallon of syrup, we must work continuously at the boiling and filtering once the season starts."

Then he paused, as if some new thought was surging in his mind for adequate expression. Looking up a moment later, he added, with a wistful smile: "Most French cooking would lose its appetizing taste without the flavor of maple syrup."

Spring with its sweet moist air invites the father to resume work in his little garden. Vegetables he plants — carrots, onions, and the other common varieties; more particularly he looks early to his perennials. Flowers seem to share the emotions of the French people — especially blooms with deep, gorgeous coloring. God exhibits in blossoms more mysterious color shades than Rembrandt ever dreamed; He displays in their complicated shapes more unsolved geometrical problems than Euclid ever imagined. Sweet williams with their scalloped petals of white and red; little pansy faces that peek from beneath wimples of every sunset shade; and stately delphinium plumes of blue which the mothers and children carry in armfuls to church on a Sunday in June to place at the feet of the Virgin's statue become emissaries that speak the prayers of their pious thoughts. The French home has a natural coziness that makes for contentment.

New Year's celebrations top the list of family social events. The inhabitants visit one another, going from one home to another, even the men kissing as they offer the greeting of the day. After punch is served, the host follows to the next stopping place. The day is made one long, memorable occasion. Devotion to St. Anne, the mother of the Virgin Mary, assumes wide church significance with religious festivities on July 26. Regular daily attendance at services during Holy Week, although not required, is still practiced. Several French communities in Northern Wisconsin observe occasions commemorative of Joan of Arc, the French heroine.

The Wisconsin French Canadian farmer is easygoing and thrifty, like the habitant of the Quebec province. Rarely does he seek help and seldom does he ask for charity. He is never hurried nor excited and has a capacity and willingness for work. But he is always ready to take time off for visits and often packs up the family and, his conveyance loaded with food and drink, goes to spend the day with a neighbor in merrymaking. French children invariably wear blue or red ribbons in their hair or around their necks; the women are fond of dress and jewelry and their appearance is usually pleasing. Rug weaving and the making of fancy quilts, either for gain or pastime, are carried on within many of the homes. Some of the men play the violin for family dancing or for evening amusements. Many of the French Canadians whom I met have a strong dash of Indian blood, which they don't like to admit. [6]

"All the other French families round about are part Indian, except my family" was a customary answer to my inquiries.

Their sons are patriotic, preferring to enlist in the navy. A chance to see the world satisfies their roving dispositions. The Somerset French settlement claimed the distinction in World War II of furnishing more men to the navy than any other community of its size in the United States.

Four generations of life in Wisconsin have not eliminated the sharp inflection given to the pronunciation of many English words nor removed, from ordinary conversation, expressions that sound odd though literally translated from the mother tongue. Characteristic among the French Canadian is an emphasis on the last syllable so that "Frenchman" is pronounced as "French *man*" and "high school" as "high *school*"; or they precede words beginning with a vowel with the letter "h" so that "oil" is articulated as if it were spelled "hoil" and "air" as "hair." Among the less educated "she" is commonly used after masculine nouns — "Mrs. Demarse said of her dull boy: 'My son Dolph, she funny boy' " Expressions that are perfect in French become awkward when translated into English: "Me, I do not know him" (Moi je ne le connais pas), or "You, are you crazy, you?" (Vous, etes vous fou?). Among these people I found that parents speak the native language to their children when they do not want strangers to know what they are saying. Otherwise, English is used in conversation around the home. Less frequent every year are the occasions for songs and recitations in French at school programs and entertainment.

Of all the French villages in Wisconsin, Somerset, a community in St. Croix County, within sight of the distant smoke of Stillwater, and noted for its frog farms, alone remains with many Old World customs "unspoiled." Religion means much to these people. A church to St. Anne, whose shrine east of Quebec is probably the most celebrated on the continent, spiritualizes their lives. The bell is rung at baptisms to announce the advent of a new parishioner. It is tolled regardless of the time of the day, but not at night, six times for a female and nine times for a male, to inform the community of a death.

"This ringing is a request for a prayer for the deceased," explained Father W. A. Beaudette, a fourth generation Acadian. His great-grandfather was a youthful member of the Grand Pre communities when the British dispersion of 1757 occurred, a story immortalized by Longfellow in "Evangeline."

"In rural communities, usually everyone knows who is very sick," continued the pastor.[7] "The difference in the number of the ringings has no other significance than to distinguish the sex. It is a custom brought to the Western World from France in 'the reign of the Henrys.' Except also for several French settlements in the Chippewa Valley, I doubt if any other localities in the United States have preserved this custom. At wakes there is little sitting around and eating. Instead, prayers are said in common for fifteen minutes, commencing every hour on the hour."

I could not help feeling that the veneration shown by their young people to age is a lost virtue among Americans that might profitably be revived to insure greater love and stability in family circles. Children and grandchildren kneel for grandfather's New Year's blessing. He places a hand on each bowed head and usually with wet eyes says an improvised prayer over the kneeling child. The scene is one of those rare touches in human affairs — as when a busy crowd falls back to let a baby's funeral pass.

While the romantic, religious days are fast leaving the lives of the French in Wisconsin, their devotion, respect, courtesy and hospitality to Old World ideals continue as inherited traits.

[1] Wisconsin folk songs were collected under the direction of the University of Wisconsin School of Music during 1940-41 and placed in the archives of the Library of Congress, Washington, D. C. A French school teacher in Green Bay sang the songs of her ancestors to be recorded.

[2] A silver soleil (or ostensorium) given by Nicholas Perrot, French commandant of the West, to St. Xavier Mission in De Pere, in 1686, is the oldest memento of French civilization in Wisconsin. It is kept in the museum in Green Bay.

[3] Sherry, Laura. **Old Prairie du Chien** (Introduction by Zona Gale), Paris, 1931, p. 15.

[4] In all these localities there are parishes requiring the services of a priest who can speak French. In French communities, especially Prairie du Chien and Green Bay, the French landholding system prevailed. Trowbridge, Frederick N., **Land Titles in Wisconsin**, Wisconsin Magazine of History, Vol. XXVI, No. 3, p. 315.

[5] Schuh, Rev. Gerald F., Souvenir History of St. Rose of Lima Congregation. Cadott, Wisconsin, 1936, p. 20.

[6] The Canadians resent American novelists making villains of mixed Canadian and Indian blood. In fact the metis—or half-blood—is usually a fine character because invariably such half-breed is a good Christian and a good citizen. This explains partially at least why they do not boast of their Indian blood. The first settlers were coureurs des bois or trappers who sought wives. The only available females were among the natives. The Indian woman made a good wife. It is doubtful if the imported white woman could have survived the hardships of the wilderness in the early days.

Rev. W. A. Beaudette.

[7] Under the subject heading of **"Bells,"** Catholic Encyclopedia, Vol. II, refers to this custom as existing back many centuries.

❖

CHAPTER II

Come, Let's Touch Pipes a Bit
Mineral Point and Linden

SAFFRON BUNS!

That improvised sign in the window of a squat little bakery that hugs the sidewalk of one of the narrow, inclined streets in Mineral Point advised shoppers that Cornish buns were on sale that Saturday. Upon me the notice burst as a surprise as I sauntered along the crowded thoroughfare — one minute distracted by tangling traffic; the next puzzled over dim letterings on the facades of century-old, stone buildings begrimed by weather. For the moment I did not understand the announcement. So I paused. At one side of the display window were pans of golden breakfast rolls. They were so different from any to which I had been accustomed that I entered the shop to inquire about them. The ancient doorway was itself a fitting entrance to the land of Lorna Doone.

"This is a Cornish community," explained the baker. "On Wednesdays and Saturdays we make a specialty of Cornish baking. Usually we had the rolls every day but since the Spanish Civil War we have been compelled to conserve our supply of saffron."

"What has the war to do with your work?" I inquired.

"Everything. All saffron comes from Spain. It is made from the powdered petals of a purple crocus plant. Until recent years it cost us only $7.00 a pound; now it is $35.00. At one time the price soared to $80.00. All local drug stores and most of the groceries carry the product, so common is the demand. Cornish people relish many of their foods flavored with this deep orange dye. To them it is a great disappointment not to have saffron breads regularly at their meals. Our baking of fifty dozen rolls lasts only a few hours."

Officials of the Wisconsin Bakers' Organization claim that Cornish bakers were the last to relinquish the custom of throwing in the thirteenth bun for steady customers who bought a dozen.

Afterwards I was to learn much about these quaint people who came to Southern Wisconsin, some as early as 1830, to work in the lead mines.[8] Their low yellowish stone houses, which have weathered beautifully, their strange customs and soft dialects are as indigenous to their settlements today, a century after their coming, as in Cornwall, England, whence they migrated.

Spring was a propitious time for my visit. Although a thaw had awakened the brooks and stained the ravine snows without melting them, from the country came only a sound of constant dripping and a hurried song of hillside waters. It was too wet for the Cornish farmers to work upon the lands. So they had leisure to discuss their forbears. But only a few of the pioneers were found to survive. In conversation they called themselves "Cousin Jacks" and referred to their ancestral home in Cornwall as if it were a nation independent of England.

"Come, let's touch pipes a bit," said the general merchant at Waldwick. We settled down in chairs around the stove in the hamlet store to talk of the past; to recount the story of this old home of the Sac and Fox Indians where the great warrior Black Hawk made his last stand; and where organized territorial government took shape in a little timber box frame building that still stands under the shadow of the pioneer landmark, Belmont Mound.

Economic conditions in the mines of Cornwall, low wages, long hours and luring stories of opportunities in the rich mines of the New World inspired the more energetic to emigrate.[9] They came first to the Galena section of Illinois, but soon invaded Southern Wisconsin, settling near Shullsburg, Mineral Point and Dodgeville. There they built homes of native stone, usually on hillsides. The walls of their houses were two feet thick, the windows deeply sunken, the doors six paneled, the floors of pine sawed in varied width, the rooms heated with two or three fireplaces. From the kitchen a door led to an underground root cellar carved out of the rock, whitewashed above and set with rows of canned fruits around the outside walls.

Discouraged American miners were abandoning their holdings, which were eagerly seized by the newcomers, whose experience turned the mines temporarily into earning properties. From 1835 to 1850, when the discovery of gold in California attracted the miners to the Pacific Coast, the Cornish immigration continued annually. Estimates fix the number that settled during that period in Iowa, Lafayette and Grant counties at 8,500. They gave impetus to mining operations around Platteville, Potosi, British Hollow, Hazel Green, New Diggings, Linden, Shullsburg, Dodgeville and Blue Mounds. When they came, the landscape was already pockmarked with holes burrowed by the miners, not unlike those made in miniature by the badger — a custom that was to give Wisconsin its nickname, the Badger State. By its scars it is still remembered.

Hills and valleys of the Southwestern Wisconsin countryside, where the Cornish mined, bear Old World names reminiscent of their nostalgic longings — Cornish Hollow, Devonshire Hollow, British Hollow and many more. Most of the Cornish were surface miners. With pick and windlass the ore was loosened and brought to the surface. It was floated down the Fever River from Galena, Illinois, to reach St. Louis, or carted across country for smelting in the shot tower at Helena, a site near Spring Green which has since been turned into a state park. The weekly newspaper at Shullsburg still wears its mining title — Pick and Gad — the state seal still enshrines the miner in historic glory, and earth scars left from early excavation still disfigure the rural scene.

"If the price of lead should suddenly triple, so as to make surface mining profitable, every Cornishman would be digging again in his back yard," declared Edwin R. Shorey, professor of mining engineering at the University of Wisconsin, who lived for years in Southern Wisconsin. "The adventurous spirit of the prospectors is in their blood."

My first feeling as I look upon this rugged country is one of genuine pleasure. I never feel at ease where the lands are flat and the views boundless. Moreover, I like to catch glimpses into the lives of others. Southwest Wisconsin, the old homes and mines of the Cornish, thrill me with delight. By an accident of geology, mineral-bearing rock, lying entirely in the "driftless area," was left exposed near the surface in the lead district. That happenstance makes primitive methods of mining successful. Besides, the wrinkled contour of the landscape bears the pristine touch of creation's dawn. I never tire of the changing vistas in this section. Easterners fondly designate it as the "Berkshire Hills."

When into such a country a people as simple and guileless as the shepherds of Bethlehem are introduced, there arises a combination of landscape and life that soon teems with legends. I have gone back, again and again, to make sure that the captivating panoramas have not disappeared in my absence. Always a visit results in opening new areas of interest among the people.

Cornish young men gather frequently in taverns to sing. The attention of bystanders augments the volume of their vociferous tones to carry such rousing strains as "Sound, Sound Your H'instruments of Joy" into the streets. " 'Ark the 'Erald Angels Sing" is a hymn that lifts their hearty voices to heights of supreme natural beauty.

Time has touched with fancy the career of at least one early Cornishman. For generosity, courage and feats of skill, the achievements of F. W. Shadick have assumed in the communities of Southwest Wisconsin the role of a Paul Bunyan. Shadick is universally known as the "Scotch Giant."[10] Before coming to America he traveled with a circus in England. Arriving in Wisconsin on the eve of its statehood he worked for several years as a teamster hauling lead between Mineral Point and Galena. The feats of brawn displayed by this colossus of a man—seven feet four and weighing 370 pounds—have become mythical traditions when retold around the evening firesides.

Afterwards Shadick joined a large western circus, where his exhibitions of strength were among the surprising advertised events. It was while performing at La Porte, Indiana, in 1854, that he was stricken and died. He is buried at Rewey.

"I have been trying for years to find a circus poster of the 'Scotch Giant,' but have never succeeded," explained James Dolan of Platteville at our last visit. "But everywhere I go among the Cornish settlements of Grant, Lafayette and Iowa counties I hear almost unbelievable tales of this Cornish Hercules."

Two succeeding generations have softened the Cornish speech. Only an occasional word, or the harsh sounding of the "h" betrays the ancestral tongue.

The story is told of an old miner trudging into Hazel Green when he was beset by a farmer's dog. Using his bag as a defense the Cornishman began to retreat.

"Jock, that dorg won't bit. E's waggin' his tail," shouted the farmer in encouragement.

"I know that," responded 'Cousin Jack.' "E's waggin' e's tail at one hend and barkin' at the hother. O doan't naw which of his hends to believe."[11]

Until the eighteenth century the Cornishman had his own language, and many stories are told of his refusal to abide by the conventions of English grammar and pronunciation.

A Cornish mother, complimented on the beaming face of her young daughter, is reputed to have replied: "Yes, 'er face do be the best limb she 'ave."

With the decline of surface mining, most of the Cornish have become farmers. Estimates fix the number of their descendants in Southern Wisconsin at 20,000. The unusually high illiteracy rate of the first Cornish has disappeared in the succeeding generations. Nevertheless, they have continued a simple people—peaceful and contented. Though conservative in political thought, few among them have aspired to office; fewer have entered the professions:

"Of manners gentle, of affections mild;
In wit, a man; Simplicity, a child."

The Cornish are predominantly Protestant.

"There isn't a Catholic church within eight miles," boasted one rural Wesleyan disciple. Scarcely a community in the mining district is not sentineled by a Methodist church spire. Following the Reformation in Cornwall, Wesleyanism enrolled a large percentage of the working classes. When these families migrated to Wisconsin, they were quick to join with American organizations holding similar views.

Some there were, however, who believed that the Wesleyans had departed from the original tenets. These united with the Primitive Methodists and founded their own churches—an otherwise little known denomination in Wisconsin.[12] A single city block separates the Primitive Methodist and the Methodist Episcopal churches in Benton and Linden. Primitive Methodists have edifices at:

> *Benton circuit*—Benton, Leadmine and Jenkinsville.
> *Platteville circuit*—Platteville and Big Patch.
> *New Diggings circuit*—New Diggings and Wardsville.
> *Linden circuit*—Linden and Mifflin.
> *Ridgeway circuit*—Ridgeway and Stannard.
> *Pleasant View circuit*—Pleasant View and Rowesville.

State compulsory education of the children has broken down many provincialisms. But the activities of the church groups have kept alive the home customs. Singularities of dress, low-crowned hats once worn by the men; caps turned inside out in "pisky laden" to keep the evil spirits from leading one astray, are now looked upon as only eccentricities. Instead, the Cornish have become crusaders against the dance hall and hard liquor and in many localities now tolerate neither of these; afternoon Ladies' Aid meetings regale their visitors with such Cornish dishes as the pasty saffron cake and clotted cream; visitors are always begged to stay and "have a dish of Tay"; the men still believe in quitting work Saturday noon and spending the after-dinner hours visiting and smoking.

Of Cornish food the pasty is the most common. Vegetables are baked like pie crust, triangular in shape, of a size to fit the pocket of the miner. There are about as many kinds of pasties as there are meats and vegetables. The pasty is the prized dish at every celebration and is served regularly at many restaurants in old lead districts, except on fast days of Lent.

It seems to me that I have never enjoyed people more than I have this year — not those who go on hurried, unseeing tour or to the lakes to spend the summer — but those who work in mines and factories and in the fields — sowing, cultivating, harvesting. My visits among them have been unhurried. Some of these were men ignorant of books but wise in the knowledge of life. One such unlettered man told me that "no man has a corner on doing things." Not until later did I grasp the full meaning of his remark; not until I thought of how determined many of his like in old countries have refused to be cornered by intolerable conditions, but rather found freedom in the New World to work out their own destinies. How few of us have the courage to pursue the lofty visions of our souls? Yet had it not been for the invasion of these aggressive European stocks the strong bedrock of Wisconsin civilization might have been more friable.

I am coming to understand the great happiness of those who dream dreams and strive for their fulfillment.

Others were shrewd to foresee the interest which the public and the tourist would take in the Cornish. Their old homes have lent a romantic tone. Max Fernekes, a Milwaukee artist, moved to Mineral Point and has found a market for his distinctive water color-crayon drawings of Cornish life among "those who have gone away." Robert Neal of Mineral Point and Edgar Hellum of Stoughton purchased adjoining limestone Cornish homes on old Shake Rag Street, which they have named the Pendarvis House. There you may enjoy a real Cornish meal featured with large helpings of pasties and plum pudding in an early day Cornish atmosphere.

Shake Rag Street and Jail Alley in Mineral Point have acquired an interest among Wisconsin tourists akin to that expressed by visitors who first see La Petite Rue Sous Le-Cap in Quebec. Local surroundings named both thoroughfares. Shake

Rag received its name from the custom of the Cornish wives shaking a cloth or dish rag from the kitchen door to call their men to dinner from the mines on the hill across the valley.

Toward the end of the year landscape and life change. The summer browns and greens of hillside and valley now lie scarved with snow. The smoke of early evening rises from two, sometimes three, fireplaces in the same sandstone home in Mineral Point. On the restless winds there is a pungent smell of fresh baking.

At one window and then another appear lighted candles; at one home after another flickering tapers prick the darkness. The red glow of the hearths throws comfort into the streets. There are merry voices at the doors; happy scenes through the windows. Capella, like a benign lantern, sparkles unnoticed through grey torn clouds. Gradually the world outside becomes as silent as the planets. Soon a soft snow is falling.

It is an old-fashioned Christmas Eve along the streets where dwell the Cornish.

---

[8] Copeland, Louis Albert, **The Cornish in Southwest Wisconsin**, Wisconsin Historical Collections, Vol. XIV, pp. 301-334.

[9] Kellogg, Louise P., **Story of Wisconsin,** Wisconsin Magazine of History, Madison, Vol. III, p. 317.

[10] From stories told to author by the late James Dolan of Platteville Wisconsin: also Wisconsin Historical Collections, Vol. XIII, p. 362.

[11] Brown, Charles E., **Cousin Jack Stories**, Wisconsin Folklore Society, Madison 1940- Davis, Susan Burdick, **Wisconsin Lore for Boys and Girls** Eau Claire, 1931, pp. 126-153.

[12] Davidson, Rev. John N., in Proceedings of State Historical Society of Wisconsin, 1899, pp. 191-192. Laxey Church, near Linden, only Manx church in America, built by immigrants from the Isle of Man, existed until 1943, when it was razed.

❖

CHAPTER III

Freiheit Ist Meine

Watertown and Sheboygan

OUT in Dodge and Jefferson counties, Wisconsin, once the Mecca of German people who sought its rich, wild lands as a refuge of freedom and a home of plenty, an Old World vocation has grown to a great national industry.

Large, red barns, long fields of corn shocks, Holstein cattle in green pastures, and spacious frame houses present a scene of modern farm prosperity. But within its home circles may be found a different activity — almost medieval in its quaint methods.

If one visits a farm in the late fall at an hour when the sun is sinking resplendently in the West and the flocks and cattle are being herded for the night, an unfamiliar call will break upon the ear:

"Woode!" "Woode!" "Woode!"

The voice is measured and slow. As the echo dies, the call is intoned again and again, softer and softer. Then all is silent.

It is the housewife using the Old World call of the goose girl for the assembling of her scattered flocks. Nowhere else in the United States is one likely to find the ancient custom of caring for the geese each morning and evening as is still practiced in this enterprising community of German Americans. Once the goose girl watched her flocks by day with the patience of the pastoral shepherds. Now wire fence enclosures and the opportunities for individual advancement in the cities have lured the goose girl away, but the flocks remain. Watertown, Wisconsin, is the center of the industry.

Whenever one visits large cities, south or east of Chicago, during the poultry season and enters exclusive clubs, the eye is likely to meet the sign: "Watertown Stuffed Geese." If one travels by train, the menu card in the railroad diner announces: "Watertown Goose."

Two distinct methods are used in the preparation of the fowl for the choice markets of the world — "stuffing" and "stall feeding."

Watertown geese have a reputation of developing the largest livers of any geese that are brought into the market. That is why Watertown stands at the head of the industry. To produce a goose of thirty pounds, with a liver weighing four pounds, is to these farmers as much an achievement as the raising of a pure bred cow that will become one of the world's greatest milkers.

Geese with oversized livers are developed by a "stuffing" process of forced feeding. The raisers call it "noodling" because a rolled pasty mixture is forced down the fowl's throat every four hours to hasten the liver growth and the fattening. The fastidious epicure knows no delicacy more tasty than "pate de fois gras" made from goose livers. Shipments of 50,000 pounds of "stuffed geese" to Eastern markets are an annual event. The demand is always greater than the supply.

"Stuffing geese is an ancient custom," declared the late Dr. William F. Whyte, for many years a practicing physician in Watertown. "In the tombs of the sacred bulls in Egypt, which are four thousand years old, I saw carved on the walls a pictorial representation of the same process which has made our Watertown farmers famous."

A slower process is employed in developing "stall fed" geese. These are placed in pens, given grain and water and allowed to eat as they desire. About 300,000 pounds of this class are sold from the locality annually. The firmness of their flesh makes them a desirable bird for food — an attractive menu offering of first class hotels. To know the method for ripening the geese for market is a German secret handed down within families and is as carefully guarded as the Trappist formula for manufacturing Oka cheese. But the raising of geese is only one of many customs that still give color and individuality to the German counties of Wisconsin.

Roughly that segment of the state with Madison as the string center of the arc and with Manitowoc County as the upper swing and South Milwaukee as the lower tangent is densely settled by the descendants of people representing every class and community of German society. The first settlers arrived as early as 1839. Some came seeking religious and civic liberty; others for the purpose of improving their economic and social status. Some were Protestants, others were Catholics and a third group, composed mostly of so-called "Forty-eighters," were "Free Thinkers." Before the migration ended, the Germans were so scattered that their settlements dotting the map of Wisconsin looked like a uniform patchwork quilt. Nearly fifty percent of the people of the state now have Teutonic blood in their veins.[13] The 1940 census showed they still led with 88,808 German-born out of a total of 288,774 for all Wisconsin foreign-born recorded that year.

People of each dialect seemed to congregate in making the earliest beginnings. A whole Catholic community — parish priest and parishioners — from Baden founded St. Nazianz in Manitowoc County, which even today is quaint for its Old World atmosphere; the largest Luxemburg settlement to be found in the United States is scattered around Port Washington; the Moravians are to be found around Ebenezer in Jefferson County; harassed Protestant Prussians re-established a free Kirchhayn and Freistadt in Washington County; and the Pomeranians and Mecklenburgers gathered in Milwaukee. Some were from the ranks of the nobility, others were tradesmen, but the greater number were farmers.

Scattered among the early German settlers were many so-called "Free Thinkers."[14] At one time this group had twenty-three societies in Wisconsin alone. Mayville had one of the leading organizations. These people were mostly "Forty-eighters" — men of culture and of means. Some had exchanged titles of nobility for their freedom. They were sympathizers with the German Liberal revolution of 1848 and were the progressive liberals of their times.

It is difficult accurately to define their dogma. They were not atheists but they held a belief in some godlike principle of nature. They spoke glibly of their followership after Thomas Paine, French thinker and American revolutionist. Some had their children baptized in "the name of the United States of America." Often at their gatherings they would display the cap of freedom on the top of the liberty pole.

"Freiheit ist meine!" they shouted.

For eighty years the little village of Thiensville on the old Milwaukee River resisted christianizing influence.[15] They had their children married without benefit of clergy. They buried their dead in the old Mequon cemetery under memorials to their name only. Rural neighbors looked askance upon these strange townsmen, calling their community "Little Paris" or "The Godforsaken Village." When a non-conformist newcomer attempted a collection for the founding of a church he was met with a double offer of the amount raised if no church be founded. Repeated efforts to establish a church failed.

Thiensville was one of the last Free-Thinker communities to yield. With the death of the pioneer, anti-religious leaders' sentiment changed. A Catholic church was started in 1919, using at first a portable altar that was shipped in by freight. Grace Lutheran church was founded in 1929. Both have increasing membership. One "die-hard" reminded me of the fact that neither church dared use a bell to herald their God.

"There is no bell because neither congregation has desired one," retorted the Lutheran pastor.

At Sauk City remains the last active Freie Gemeinde hall and library in Wisconsin. A spacious lawn and spreading trees give it the imposing setting of a rural community social center. As its members die they are buried in the nearby Free-Thinker cemetery in the Town of Honey Creek.

Settling first in the picturesque Kettle Moraine section along the Lake Michigan shore that they might enjoy an accessible market for their produce, the German farming class increased rapidly. Like the athlete ready to spring, they broke the lake shore confines. Soon the newcomers, the youngest, the best and the most hopeful of men from Old World places were moving into the inland wooded areas where they became noted as stump grubbers.[16] Once on the land, they persisted in buying out their discouraged Yankee neighbors. To handle the rich soil gave the German farmer an intuition of the future.

The better educated went into business and the professions. Soon German skilled workers — harness makers, cabinet makers, bakers, butchers, stone masons, shoemakers, cigar makers — monopolized these trades.[17] Gradually the holdings of the Germans became unified within a single area — Milwaukee, Ozaukee, Sheboygan, Manitowoc, Calumet and Dodge counties. They brought with them views on education and leadership in art, music and drama that gave to early Milwaukee the distinction of being called the "German Athens."

Meantime, among the German immigrants, leaders arose to found new industries that were to make Wisconsin known through the nation. Every German community had its brau meister. The names of Pabst, Schlitz, Blatz and Rahr became synonymous for malt beverages; Kohler for plumbing fixtures; Vollrath for porcelain enamel ware; Vits for aluminum products; Pritzlaff for wholesale hardware; Heil for oil burners; Reiss for Great Lakes coal shipments; Pfister, Vogel and Rueping for leather; Harnischfeger for heavy machinery; Lauson for tractor engines; Stoppenbach for sausage. The list might be extended indefinitely. Perhaps it is the German example of thrift that has resulted in Wisconsin attaining the second highest percentage of home ownership in the United States.

Milwaukee's vocabulary is still replete with adopted German words and expressions. Hannah Jacobson found the city's dialect sufficiently unusual to furnish her theme for a B. A. degree thesis at the University of Wisconsin. She discovered "Ach" being used as an exclamation in everyday speech. Many Milwaukee children say "tante" for "aunt"; "the streetcar bends (turns) the corner"; people "stay to home" (zu hause) instead of "stay at home"; "I go by my aunt's house" instead of "I go to my aunt's house"; "make my apron shut" is a current idiom for the English "tie my apron"; "nix come eraus" is a customary byword for "nichts kommt heraus"; "set yourself down" is a translation of the request "setzen Sie sich nieder" and "Aufwiedersehen," a friendly farewell word, may be overheard on any Milwaukee street corner as companions part to go different ways.

Near the turn of the century, with the discontinuance of language papers and the decline in the preaching of sermons in German, many of the cities began to lose their Old World flavor. The change is less noticeable in rural communities.

"Watertown remains gloriously obstinate," remarked Frank C. Blied, Madison, President of the National Turnverein. "It refuses to yield to every whim and fashion. So long as Northwestern College continues to teach the beauty of the German language and the citizens there and round about have respect for the ideals of the pioneers; so long as housewives feed their families good wholesome German cooking; and the name of Carl Schurz, who lived there, is revered as a great German American, Watertown will be distinctive."

Centuries will not efface the stamp that the Almighty placed on the face and form of the Wisconsin German farmer. The roundness and redness of countenance, the thickness and muscularity of limbs, the measured roll and slowness of gait, the industry and thrift in habits, and the affability of greeting — these are indelible characteristics. The love of song and the jovial sociability enjoyed around the board sipping beer are traits of age-long breeding.

"Sprechen sie Deutsch?" was asked of the newcomer to the cardtable at Otto's Inn, Watertown. What a wreath of smiles went around when "Ja" came as the answer.

"Essen ist fertig," announced the hausfrau a few minutes later. All hurriedly arose to enter the dining room. One glance at the savored, steaming food foretold a difference.

The German housewife has contributed more variety to the Wisconsin meal than has any other nationality. After the dinner I talked with the cook.

"Sauerkraut is the most popular of German dishes," she explained. "During the war we were asked to call it 'Liberty Cabbage,' but our guests could never become accustomed to the new name. Other favorite German dishes are cole slaw, dill pickles, potato salad, sour meats, hasenpfeffer, hamburger steak, goulash, noodles, pickled green beans, celeriac, chives, cheese cake, poppyseed rolls, pretzels, coffee cake, caraway rye and pumpernickel bread."

German bakers and delicatessen stores[18] are common in all the larger cities in the section. In Milwaukee the streets around such restaurants as Mader's, Fritz Gust's, and Old Heidelberg, any day in summertime, may display license plates from nearly every state in the Union. The fame of delicious soups flavored with onion, of spanferkel and sauerkraut, of goose with cranberry sauce, is known to every tourist entering the state. Hausfrauen in cities and country jealously treasure special recipes for cooking or making pastries. Some of the larger bakeries maintain rural delivery routes to supply customers with foods baked the German way.

"You should see my windows before Christmas," challenged R. A. Radtke, a Watertown baker. "I had cookies and cakes of all sizes, colors, tastes and designs. My, it was beautiful! And everybody wants a loaf of good old-fashioned dark rye bread."

When visiting Watertown during the holidays, I usually make purchases of German Christmas candies. Using an Old World process, Herman Kramp, the baker and candy maker, has built an extensive trade selling mazipan. Cast in the miniature design and color of all common fruits and vegetables — apples, pears, plums, peaches, carrots, peas, beets, grapes and other garden products — this delicacy made of an almond paste sells at almost a dollar a pound. Not only is it bought quite extensively in the so-called German section, but there is a slowly increasing mail trade from other states. The decorated Christmas tree is a German custom, which some attribute to Martin Luther.

A "little Germany" was once the dream of the immigrants from the fatherland who came to Wisconsin. They wanted a place where their culture could remain pure and develop unhampered. The same hope was cherished for Missouri, Illinois and Texas. But the pressure of other nationalities for the coveted lands shattered the illusion.[19]

Watertown is proud of its Old World culture and customs. Carl Schurz, who came there in 1855, gave it national political distinction.[20] His wife, Margarethe Schurz, founded there the first kindergarten system in America. Their old homesite has been appropriately marked. The Turner Gymnastic Association is still maintained, although it has taken on larger social aspects and among the men skat has never surrendered to chess, bridge or poker.

"Where is John?" was an overheard inquiry at a large hardware store on a busy Saturday afternoon.

"Down at Turner's playing cards," responded the clerk. The prospective customer examined his watch and started off in the direction of the hall.

The monthly Watertown Pig Fair is a mere transposition of the Viehmarkt in a New World environment. Founded in 1850 by Leopold Kadisch at Watertown, it was conducted, until the advent of the automobile, as a cattle fair. Now it is a gathering place on the second Tuesday of each month for the sale of vegetables, pigs, poultry, and dogs. The institution has more than a sectional reputation. Farmers come from Iowa, Illinois and Minnesota to buy. It requires the streets of five blocks to display the offerings from trucks and trailers.

"It's a busy show for about five hours and the farmer-traders vanish again," explained a local livestock buyer. "Sometimes there will be over 500 cars and probably 3,000 people milling about, visiting in German with their neighbors. Total sales for the day average from $3,000 to $5,000, depending on the season."

October brings the largest gathering. Then, in addition to the other farm products, trucks piled high with small bundles of herbs — thyme, dill, sage, basil, sweet marjoram, lavender, catnip and wormwood — are eagerly sought out by housewives, who use the dried leaves and seeds for flavoring sauces, soups and vegetables, for perfuming linens, and as a home remedy for common ailments. During the winter months fresh meats, home-made sausages and canned vegetables find a ready sale on the market.

There bargaining is an art. Many of the traders are colorful individuals — jolly, keen to discern a possible purchaser. There is good-natured but sharp banter, but the German farmer appears in a favorable role pointing and praising the superior character of his produce. Even the children, who often accompany their parents, join in explanation of the fine traits of a pig or dog they have assisted in raising. But it is as a market for small pigs that the transplanted institution claims renown. At the spring sales as many as a thousand spanferkel change hands.

I am glad that I saw all this. The memory of these distinguished habits of country life, that are slowly passing, hangs in my mind like a lovely old picture. Many older residents regret the declining use of the German language.

"Maybe in another hundred years people in this section will no longer speak German," remarked one of the pioneers after telling the story of his success in placing his five sons and daughters on farms. "But the customs will never die. They belong to the race."

That part of Wisconsin sandwiched between Madison and Lake Michigan, where the Germans predominate, was sculptured by the glaciers millions of years ago. Fertile earth and gravel beds were carted long distances on ice sheets to be spread over the area. Hills were laid low and deep valleys uplifted. When the first settlers arrived all was a rolling landscape of green trees and lush grasses. Today it is the heart of America's dairyland, with Plymouth as the nation's center of the American cheese industry. Singular as it may seem, the German sections of the state rank high in cheese output; the Scandinavian localities, in butter production.

There is something about this rich farming country contoring around Dodge County that speaks the voice of the land. Over the summer loiterer it throws the perfume of growing things. The warm air drifts lazily, yet jubilantly. Long vistas of green peas — for which Wisconsin ranks first — decorated often with blue-flowered fields of flax exult in the yellow sunshine. As evening approaches and the gladiolus shades and warmth of the receding sun bathe the sky and countryside, the tired horses, chains jangling, come down the lane followed by a weary driver and trailed by the faithful dog. A farm youth hurries across the road to release the crowding, restless cattle from the pasture lot.

Soon the air from the barns is delicious with the sweet aroma of the milking. Wisconsin is doing its farm chores.

"The best farm orchards are in German communities," a leading Wisconsin nurseryman confided. "That is because the German women water, loosen the earth and mulch the trees in summer. If left to the men-folk, their orchards might suffer the neglect of many others."

Cider mills flourish in German communities. Farmers haul their apples to the presses at Millhome, Beaver Dam, Meeme, Spring Valley, Reeseville and Rockville in much the same way as their ancestors took their grains for grist and flour. Some of the most popular cider in the state comes from the Sheboygan-Manitowoc area. And the old homemade brand of vinegar is still a common product, its making supervised by the hausfrau.

The end of summer brings a gradual respite from arduous work. October, with its golden days and hazy blue atmosphere, is signalized in some German communities with a harvest festival held on the first Sunday of the month. For forty-five years such an event has been observed annually in Sheboygan and Milwaukee by the Bavarian societies. Less regularly but over a longer period smaller German settlements have kept up the custom. It is a Thanksgiving event, religious in background, colorful with Old World civic ceremonials. Among the older Germans it is still known as the "Munchener October Fest." The day begins with the people going to church; after noon there is a parade of gaily decorated vehicles around the public square. "Das Munchener Kindl," the queen chosen for the occasion, appears dressed in white, riding on a gorgeous float at the head of the procession. She carries with her a large white radish, the symbol of the good crops which have been gathered during the harvest season. After the exhibits have passed comes the feasting — sausages, bread or rolls, beer and large cookies made of gingerbread dough, called "Leb Kuchen." To the music of either band or accordion, men and women dressed in native garb spend the evening dancing the "Schuchplattler." The whole day is made auspicious with family reunions and homecomings.

Sheboygan especially abounds with fine, old German customs. When the worker comes home in the evening, some member of the family hurries out, while the supper is being put on the table, to get a pail of beer. All enjoy this beverage with the meal. If it is summer, before retiring, the family is likely to adjourn to the back yard, where a fire is kindled in the grate and bratwurst is roasted to be served with rye bread and beer. The cool night air from Lake Michigan wafts the pleasing aroma of the open-air kitchen like an incense through the residential district.

The first touch of real cold weather ushers in an industry peculiarly adapted to the German home — the preparation and the curing of the winter meats. If a grandmother is still living in the home, it is her task to do the supervising of the making. Laying aside her spinning, she arranges all her herbs and spices on the kitchen table before she permits the delicate work of mincing the meat, seasoning and packing to proceed. German home-cured meats have a taste and flavor that the most fastidious technique used by the big packers has never been able to approach. Bratwurst packed and sold in the local meat shops of Jefferson, Beaver Dam and Sheboygan is so pleasing to Germans that once eaten no other brand will satisfy. Garlic bologna and pickled pig's feet, blood sausage and head cheese prepared by Old World methods have a special appetizing tang. The hams and bacon cured over a hickory-fire smoke by farmers and processors at Waterloo and Jefferson are marketed all through the Middle West. Squab raising is also a specialty, with Watertown leading in Mississippi Valley sales.

Among Germans the tavern is a community club house. After church, the whole family, before returning to the farm, is likely to enter to drink beer, while sitting around a table talking with friends and neighbors. These taverns are different in atmosphere from the crowded bar familiar to other communities. They have the attributes of family sociability rather than commercial activity.

Cutting a rowen crop of alfalfa, community silo filling, and husking of the fall open again opportunities for getting together. October brings the usual farm sales occasioned by changes of tenants and owners. German fathers generally collect the wages of their children until they are twenty-one years, but the money is later used to start the young folk in farming.

The fall auctions become a place to outfit the son or daughter with stock, as well as a popular gathering place for German neighbors to talk of their plans and hopes. A promised lunch of beer, sandwiches and doughnuts attracts crowds like moths to a candle light. While inspecting the machinery, there is plenty of opportunity for visiting and the whole gossip of the community comes to a focus. Now and then amid all this sundry babbel and commotion, a grandfather may be seen resting — sitting unconcerned on the tongue of a plow or wagon — peacefully smoking. I cannot put down all I saw at those auctions but I do recall the serenity of these remaining pioneers. Undisturbed, the old man puffs at his big bow-like China pipe, curving down under his chin, and capped with a perforated tin cover that reminded me of a locomotive spark catcher in the North Wisconsin logging country, as if life should be mostly a matter of comfort when one grows old. As I turned away, I remembered that the Poet Goldsmith, meditating such a scene, wrote:

"A youth of labor with an age of ease."

The apex of sociability is reached, however, after the Sunday church service. A weekday deserted crossroads like Freistadt, with its imposing Trinity Lutheran church and school, requires an officer to handle the traffic.[21] Among the people of Wisconsin, Lutherans and Catholics claim the record for church attendance. Most of these communities have also their own parochial schools where German is taught. In some places so few are the children neither Lutheran nor Catholic that the public authorities make arrangements with the church schools to furnish the necessary instruction required by law.[22]

During World War I, attempts to stir up racial hatred were carried to an absurdity. Such words as Mannerchor, Frohsim, and Liederkranz were dropped. Banks changed their names to escape a German title, the teaching of the German language was discontinued in many high schools, and the popularity of German classics declined at the University of Wisconsin. When the shadow of World War II swung across America, a Wisconsin editor, remembering the past, voiced this plea for sanity:[23]

"We've got the best of the German civilization here in America. Let's treasure the names of Mendelssohn, Schiller, Goethe, Mozart, Heine, Schubert, Strauss, Beethoven, Handel, and Bach. Let's keep them alive, and absorb them in what may be the ultimate distinctively American civilization.

"Why, you can't be properly formally married in America unless Mendelssohn or Wagner officiates! Who would give up Schubert's 'Song of Love' without defending it against bombs and tyranny? What would we do without Beethoven's 'Fifth Symphony,' Bach's 'Jesu, Joy of Man's Desiring,' Handel's 'Hallelujah' Chorus, and Schubert's 'Ave Maria'?

"Perhaps the finest gesture we could make at a time like this would be to place the missing statue of Carl Schurz on the big pedestal in that circle of heroes at Gettysburg. It is the only empty niche which is left unfilled because New York and Wisconsin got into a quarrel, each claiming Carl Schurz as its citizen."

Custom seems to have dedicated Sunday afternoon to the German family. Driving through the rural section, it is not uncommon to see a dozen cars with visiting relatives at one farm home. During the summer season the public parks are crowded on Sundays with family reunions. At Watertown and Sheboygan reservations are made with the authorities six months in advance for the use of grounds and tables. And when the day arrives it's a great event for the old folk — grandfathers talking German and smoking big bowled meerschaum pipes, and grandmothers, their Sunday dresses buried in big white aprons, sitting rather uneasily as they look on — listening to the stories of old, recalling the faces departed:

"Pleasure is the flower that fades,
Remembrance is the lasting perfume."

Men are free when they love their home. Farm beautification has been inculcated by German instinct. Old World vocations of gardening, vine culture, and horticulture have not been neglected.

"If you see a plot of beautiful flowers in the dooryard you can be almost certain that it is the home of a German farmer," a county agricultural agent interposed while giving me instructions for contemplated home visits.

And there were red geraniums and blue scabiosa in nearly every bed.

---

[13] 47.9 percent, according to census of 1930.

[14] Bruce, William George, **Memoirs**, Wisconsin Magazine of History, Vol. XVII, pp. 5-6.

[15] Milwaukee Journal, October 13, 1940.

[16] Schafer, Joseph, **The Yankee and Teuton in Wisconsin**, Wisconsin Magazine of History, Madison, Vol. VI, p. 271.

[17] Lacher, J. H. A., **The German Element in Wisconsin**, Chapter XXX Vol II. Quaife, Milo M., **Wisconsin, Its History and Its People**, Chicago (1924), pp. 153-206.

[18] A German word that means delicious eats: Mears, Louise W., "Milwaukee: A City of Good Foods," Wisconsin Magazine of History, June, 1941.

[19] Ross, Dr. E. A., **The Old World in the New, New York**, 1914, p. 50; Snyder H. M., **The Foreign Population of Wisconsin**, 1920, thesis for Ph.D. degree, University of Wisconsin, pp. 12-15.

[20] Schafer, Dr. Joseph, **Carl Schurz, Militant Liberal**, Madison, 1930, p. 74: Easum, Chester Verne, **The Americanization of Carl Schurz**, Chicago, 1929, pp, 162-258; Whyte, William F., in Vol. IV, Wisconsin Magazine of History, No. 3, March, 1921.

[21] Milwaukee Journal, October 6, 1940, **Freistadt, Haven for Religious Freedom**. Historically, the early settlers of Kirchhayn and Freistadt were known as "Old Lutherans" because they migrated to America to preserve, inviolate from government interference, their religious beliefs. See Everest, Kate A., **Early Lutheran Immigration to Wisconsin**, Trans. Wisconsin Academy of Sciences, Arts and Letters, Vol. VIII, 1891.

22 Roxbury, Dane County.

23 Brayton, A. M., **An American Apostle's Creed**, Wisconsin State Journal, Madison, December 28, 1941.

❖

CHAPTER IV

Spire Guides Luxemburgers
Port Washington

I T was years before I realized that in the German-speaking northeastern part of Ozaukee County existed a community that in reality was not settled by Germans at all. The people spoke a dialect of German. Like many Germans, they had large families. They exhibited all the industry and frugality of Germans. They were surrounded, like the Grand Duchy of their ancestors in Europe, by German neighbors. But they were not Germans; they were Luxemburgers.

St. Mary's spire on the hill at Port Washington lifts itself above the Lake Michigan harbor like a phantom lighthouse designed in stone and anchored for eternity. It has been the unfailing Luxemburg beacon for direction and faith. Six families of Luxemburgers came to that vicinity in 1848. Where Luxemburgers go first, others follow, just as where Catholics settle there soon arises a church. The country in Europe from which they came is almost wholly Catholic. These settlers hailed from the Grand Duchy proper — from what is left of the Grand Duchy after three partitions — and from the former grand-ducal territories, chiefly the province of Luxemburg in Belgium from which the townships of Belgium and Belgian Station on the old Milwaukee Lake Shore Road took their names. Politically these latter immigrants were Belgian, but racially, culturally, and linguistically they were and still are Luxemburgers.

The communities of Port Washington, Lake Church, Fredonia, Dacada, Holy Cross and Belgium in Ozaukee and Sheboygan counties, and Luxemburg in Kewaunee County, where the descendants of Luxemburger immigrants still live, remain

Catholic. Outside of these limits, one finds many Luxemburgers but not in the same compactness. Ozaukee County, the cradle of their colonization in this country, derives its name from the Indian word "red earth," an indigenous characteristic of the rich soil where first they settled.

When the first families arrived they were reluctant to pre-empt more than 40 acres of land. That seemed such a large farm compared to the crowded plots then tilled by the wealthier landlords in old Luxemburg that it was beyond their wildest dreams to contemplate more extensive holdings. But after the trees were felled and the wild lands were brought under plow there was little remaining for these large families, numbering from twelve to eighteen children, to do several months of each year. Further immigration became inevitable. Many of the sons of the pioneers moved westward to homesteads in Iowa, Minnesota and the Dakotas. Those remaining acquired the surrendered areas which became the foundations of the large Ozaukee County farms operated today by the descendants of Luxemburgers. One native trait still persists. Some observers call it their competitive instinct, others identify it as envy. Whatever designation may be given, the truth is that between the men folks there is a constant rivalry to see who can excel in crops, production, and advancement. There are no sluggards among them.

Although three generations removed from the founders, the Old Country dialect is still preserved in its purity. Store clerks in Port Washington must be able to conduct an entire shopping conversation in the Luxemburger language. North of Port Washington, along Lake Michigan, and for some miles into Sheboygan County, there is farm after farm where I heard only the sound of the native Luxemburg speech.

"Giss! Giss! Giss!" is an old Luxemburger call occasionally heard morning, noon and night as the farmer summons the swine. And how the pigs do come at the sound of that hissing voice, kicking up a cloud of dust in the pastures as they hurry to the feeding troughs!

Luxemburg farmers are modern in their farm operations. But

in these days of mechanical improvements there is one garden tool made and used by them that I found among no other immigrant group. It was a heavy hoe, more like a pick-ax, that could be used for grubbing and loosening the earth. Even their gardens have a strange variety. There are some vegetables and plants seldom grown elsewhere — shallots, chives and wormwood.

"Wormwood is the herb that has cured the illness of many a pioneer," volunteered the aged Catholic priest, Rev. John J. Pierron of Burlington, whose parents were among the first Luxemburg-Ozaukee arrivals, as he pointed to the thrifty, green plant (to me more of a garden weed). He explained that it is often known as bitter balsam.

"There isn't a Luxemburg family that would do without it," he continued. "The leaves may be steeped as a tea or mixed with whiskey and used as a medicine. It is prescribed for stomach ailments."

Father Pierron explained that the Luxemburgers are a quiet people with a genuine love for the traditions of their ancestors. This is their way of life, preferred by them to the hurry, confusion and insecurity found in urban districts.

"At least three words have been contributed by the Luxemburgers to the English language," he added. "The word 'little' comes from the Luxemburg word 'letzel,' as in 'letzelburg,' meaning a small fortress; the word 'cabbagehead' from 'kalbesheid,' being pronounced similarly in both languages, and 'home' from the same word as in 'sommerhome,' a name borne for centuries by a shady residence."

No other nationality group I have visited employs nicknames so universally to identify their friends and kinsmen as do the Luxemburgers. The Norwegians frequently adopt the farm name of their ancestral home; the Irish are prone to satirize their companions and neighbors with some appellation suggestive of a predominant personal trait or characteristic. But the Luxemburgers use a variety of identification methods. One may be better known by the added family name of his father-in-law than by his own; or he may bear the name of the community from which his ancestors immigrated; or be designated by some deformity of nature; or by some religious or political tenet espoused.

Such a variety of nicknames are employed that a "Dictionary," or "Self Identifier of Names Applied to the Inhabitants of the Northern Part of Ozaukee County" was compiled and issued in 1908 by N. E. Becker of Dacada. It is still in use, but a revised edition is presently needed. It contains more than 1,000 nicknames. Among the characteristic ones are:

> Jenn Becher — right name Johann Schumacher — his wife came from Bech, he didn't.
> Grosen Bescher (Big Bescher) — right name Nikolas Mart.
> Pitt Donver — right name Peter Schneider — wife came from Donven.
> Skinny Watry, a brother of Cripple Watry.
> Big Berend, Big Joseph, Big Lorenz, Big Nick, Big Oswald, Big Schuster, Big Weiland, Big Weinand — because of their height.
> Petchen Kalks (lime) — right name Peter Graf — name came from his ownership of a stone quarry.
> Cannon Mueller — right name Andrew Mueller — had served in artillery.
> Machine Jenn — right name Johann Kelten — built thresh machines.
> Plaster John, Sponge John, Prussian Frank, Brains John (the butcher), Talkative Hanz, Goldsmith Jenn, Black Jake — because of their habits or occupations.

The coming of the Luxemburgers to Wisconsin is a story not only of migration but of spiritual adventure, it is a seeking not only of new lands but of a place where their customs and beliefs might flourish undefiled by meddlesome neighbors. They draw a proud line of distinction between themselves and other peoples who speak a similar tongue.

Some present day Luxemburgers live in stone houses built by their great-great-grandfathers. They find their pleasures at home and in community affairs. Dacada boasts of a 92-year record without a mixed religious marriage. Their young people like to dance. Young and old dunk their doughnuts in their coffee at their festivals. The old life has become an idyll.

"Musz treipen" is a sausage made and eaten with evident relish during the fall and winter. It is a mixture of the blood, lungs and livers of animals, seasoned with garden herbs and made bulky by adding chopped cabbage. Before being served it is boiled and then fried. Rutabagas and turnips also are favorite dishes at the noonday meal.

Port Washington, the "capital" of Luxemburgland, has a national reputation for its fish dinners.

It is the chance things in pilgrimages that appear to be significant. Eating a meal with a family often reveals more about the life of the people than weeks of casual association. Cooking is an art which domestic science teachers can approach only by the degrees of actual experience. Luxemburg mothers hold post-graduate honors in the School of the Kitchen Stove. Large families make eating a home problem of prime importance. Cooking and baking big meals thrice daily afford a practice to Luxemburg mothers that perfects the knack. By constant trials they gain the guerdon of being recognized as excellent cooks which many housewives with fewer children to feed have never achieved. Sometimes I think it would be to the advantage of the community if some of these mothers, who may even not be able to speak English correctly, were to be invited in for a week to take charge of high school classes in culinary training. Pupils might forget the instructions given them about measuring and weighing, but they would learn something about flavoring, broiling and baking that would make the simplest meal a remembrance as unforgettable as good music. Luxemburg mothers need no trained cooking school experts to suggest a menu for the next meal; no radio adviser to tell them how to spend their spare time. Sunday is their day for such visits, rest, and relaxation as the family cases will permit.

Many of the oldest members of these Ozaukee inland rural communities have never seen a motion picture show. When representatives of the Royal family have come among them, they have entertained them at the churches. In their settlement public relief is almost unknown. They are few in number — probably 10,000 — but they are magnanimous in spirit. History has often recorded that a small people acquires greatness by steadfastness in suffering and adherence to high ideals. The Wisconsin Luxemburgers have kept both their faith and their ideals.

At summer picnics and family gatherings the favorite song is "Zur Erenneronk" (for remembrance). All twelve stanzas are usually sung in order to recall the story of the early settlement, the clearing of the land, and how, with prosperity, they now have money in the bank and mortgages on the property of others. St. Nicholas day (December 6) is annually observed in churches and homes, and there is scarcely a family in the community that does not have a son bearing the surname of this patron saint of the children.

When I visit the Luxemburgers, which I usually do each summer, I become subtly conscious of the centuries of simple living reflected in their daily lives.

"A Luxemburger who persists in evil ways must soon move elsewhere," commented an observant outsider, who moreover has represented them in various governmental capacities during half a century. "The recreant usually does this without suggestion because he has been ostracized already."

Although in their New World surroundings the Luxemburgers operate farms that produce abundant harvests, there is nothing meretricious about them. They make their homes on a curve-contoured landscape sculptured ages ago by vanished immigrant glaciers, and have continued to live as not to break with the ancient past. The Ozaukee County community thrives as a bit of the Grand Duchy of Luxemburg.

❖

CHAPTER V

Festive Vikings Devour Lutefisk
Stoughton and Westby

T HE nostalgia of exiled peoples has enriched the world of music and literature. I sensed this keenly one evening as I approached a vine-festooned farm home in the tobacco district of Southern Dane County and heard from the open window the soft tones of a monochord. It touched me as the vibrant appeal of a lonely heart.

Early taught to sing the psalms to the music of the one-stringed salmodikon, Norwegian daughters of Wisconsin have carried this Old World custom to heights of folk festival glory. With it, family quartets awaken dreams of the native land at homecomings and at special church events. Before the advent of the organ, the salmodikon was used to lead the singing in the churches and for teaching to school children the melodies of the hymns. Stoughton has many who still play it with that richness of tone that must have awakened the lonely hearts of the pioneers. One quartet from McFarland has attracted wide attention on the folk festival programs conducted at state fairs, the Century of Progress at Chicago, and three national folk gatherings in Washington.

"When originally played, only one string was employed," said Mrs. Elsie Thompson, leader of the McFarland group. "With my two daughters and niece to assist, we believe we have improved the system by playing four salmodikons in ensemble, something that was never done in Norway."

Descendants from the land of the fjords touch hands across oceans with their ancestors. Three out of four persons met on the streets of Westby or Stoughton — outstanding centers of transplanted Norwegian culture — speak Norwegian; they dance the "halling" at weddings and Christmas celebrations; they send their sons and daughters to St. Olaf's College in Minnesota for higher education; they travel long distances to participate in annual Norwegian sangerfests; and they celebrate the "Syttende Mai" on May 17 in observance of Norway's Independence.

The Norwegians arrived early in Wisconsin, and now their blood courses in the veins of at least ten percent of the population.[24] Numerically, they are outnumbered only by the Germans and the Poles; the 1940 census showed 23,211 foreign-born Norwegians compared with 31,487 Poles. Ole K. Nattestad was the first Norwegian to come, settling in Rock County in 1830; what was to become the historic Lake Muskego settlement of Waukesha and Racine counties was started the year following; and the famous Koshkonong colony of southeastern Dane County was founded in 1840. By 1850 about seventy per-cent of the Norwegians in the United States were living within the state. The Vernon County group between the Kickapoo Valley and the Mississippi River, from Viroqua to Westby, has retained its old ways better than all others, although dispersing offspring in all possible directions.

Today, every county in Wisconsin has a Norwegian settlement. The three principal concentrated areas, however, are: first, in Rock, Walworth and Racine counties in Southwestern Wisconsin; second, in Dane, Jefferson, Columbia, Lafayette and Iowa counties in the Central part of the state; and third, in Vernon, Crawford, La Crosse, Jackson. Trempealeau, Eau Claire, Dunn and Pierce counties along the Mississippi River. Dane County Norwegians lead all other nationalities; Door County has, at Ephraim, the single Scandinavian Moravian community.[25] The University of Wisconsin claims distinction as the only American university where Norwegian has been taught continuously for as long as three-quarters of a century.

While the earlier Norwegian emigrants were primarily tillers of the soil, in recent years the descendants have become increasingly active in manufacturing, trade and professional callings. The two most important tobacco centers in Wisconsin, each with a million dollar crop annually, coincide with the state's two outstanding Norwegian settlements. Westby is the commercial center of one, Stoughton the hub of the other.

Time has spread the indescribable glamour of age over the twisting roads and rolling hills of the early Muskego community.[26] Here was built in 1843 the first church by Norwegians in America, since moved and preserved as a shrine on the campus of Luther Seminary at St. Anthony Park, Minneapolis; here were founded the first two Norwegian newspapers in America; here was the focus of early Norwegian culture, out of which have come great men and great memories; here has been dedicated the historic Heg Memorial Park in remembrance of the organizer of the famous Fifteenth Regiment, made up of Norwegians who fought bravely in more than twenty battles of the Civil War. Here is an epic story worthy of telling.

Puzzled by the conflicting names on the old tombstones in the Muskego Norwegian cemetery, I sought an explanation. Then it was that I learned of a phenomenon in family nomenclature which has gradually merged into American ways. Successive visitations of cholera brought many early burials to this ground, and, as a rule, the first markers erected gave the full church or "gaard" name of the victim, together with dates and other family data, such as "Udvandret fra Lier, 1842," literally "outwandered from Lier, 1842." Often at the bottom would be a biblical quotation or a stanza from a hymn. The softer marble stones with their precious inscriptions may be found piled up as a border fence —

"Unregarded age in corners thrown."

Replacing them will be found the more imposing granite blocks, monuments less to the dead than to the salesmanship of monument makers, or to the pride of family or birth.

But in the settlement days and afterwards, while Norwegian was still generally spoken, I was to discover that it was not uncommon for a man to be known by three names. First, he would have his church name. This would be purely Norwegian and often would be the name of the farm he had come from in Norway. But such names would often be unpronounceable to Americans, such as "Ornehaugen," meaning Eaglehill, or "Bjaadland," or "Bjelde."

Then there would be his American name for the purpose of business, for the tax assessor and the census enumerator. This American name might be Nelson, Johnson or Anderson. Lastly, among intimate friends and acquaintances generally he might have a more familiar name suggesting some distinction or peculiarity, such as "Black Ole," "Little Hans," or "Torbjorn Looking Glass," which was bestowed upon one pioneer dandy who carried a small mirror that he might "look at himself" occasionally.

On Highway 51, three miles east of Stoughton, in early days lived a Norwegian hermit in a shack. His given name was "Tomos" (Thomas). Living at a crossing of roads he was known among his Norwegian neighbors only as "Tomos Crossen" (Thomas at the crossing). Sometimes a letter would come to him addressed "Thomas Xsen." Near him was another character, also a pioneer hermit, who lived on the prairie and who was known as "Prairie Skrubben" (Prairie Wolf).

"Perfection of land titles in this country and the convenience of business have eliminated the variety of names by which one Norwegian might be known," admitted Albert O. Barton, a recognized historian of Norse immigration to Wisconsin. The Muskego settlement may be more outwardly singular in this regard but every Norwegian community can offer early examples of the confusion in names which made necessary the adoption of the American way of conferring names.

Compared to Muskego, the Koshkonong and Westby settlements are modernistic. Long rows of green tobacco in summer have made the countrysides more attractive; long red sheds crowded with curing tobacco in winter have made their owners wealthier. Politically, they have earned distinction as the bulwark of the Progressive movement which was charted under the leadership of the late Robert M. La Follette. It gave to La

Follette strength as Wisconsin's dynamic crusader against economic wrongs. The Norwegian vote of Wisconsin, Iowa and Minnesota placed Abraham Lincoln in the White House.

At the outset of my June visit in the Koshkonong settlement, my mind strayed away from the work before me on the farms, where men were removing the white muslin protection from beds of tobacco plants preparatory to planting, to thoughts of art treasures I had often seen in the homes I was passing. Woodenware, chairs and vanity boxes decorated with rosemaling are a distinctive form of Norwegian designing. Some women carry on this work in winter for amusement, when not busy with the old-fashioned type of knitting. Many homes, however, have been supplied from nearby Stoughton where Per Lysne and members of retired farm families have revived commercially this old Norwegian art.

Down in the basement of the Lysne home I found old men busy turning out the large "smorgasburd" platters; the "kubbestal" chairs made from hollowed old logs; the "bandestol" chairs with back and arms a single curved band of wood; handkerchief boxes and trays in all sizes and shapes. All over the house similar pieces decorated in bold flourishes of red and blue and made distinctive by bright delicate scrolls of green and white, were drying or awaiting to be selected. Some of these designs date back to the twelfth century.

"Rosemaling bears the same relation to the more formal Norwegian art that folk songs bear to the classic," explained Mrs. Louis Severson, pausing in her decorating to choose an added color. "It is the art of the people; that is why it has lived for centuries. These designs have become as representative of Norwegian homes as is the food we eat."

This lesson in art was an introduction to the broader understanding of the beauties of Norwegian life and culture represented when, a few months later, I visited "Little Norway," tucked away in the valleys three miles out of Mt. Horeb. Seemingly a hamlet plucked from the mountains of Norway, this estate of eighty acres and fifteen buildings of rough hewn oak is on the site of one of the pioneer Norwegian farms in the state.

Gathered in these buildings are handicrafts and antiques, from hand-carved wooden spoons, wine glasses, rugs and dishes, to great Norse chests bearing designs of artistic rosemaling.

What Williamsburg, Virginia, is as an American museum of colonial life, Isak J. Dahle sought to present to Wisconsin in creating "Little Norway" as a representation of the culture of his forbears, who were among the first settlers of the Daleyville and Mt. Horeb region. As the old pioneers of the settlement learned of the undertaking, they donated their relics. By so doing they have helped to create the largest Norwegian museum on this continent. The most attractive portion of the collection is housed in the Norway building, which was built in Norway and taken to France for the Paris exposition of 1889, then to Chicago for the fair of 1893. All buildings are typical of pioneer Norwegian architecture. Some are thatched with grass and sod; some are roofed with wide shingles hand-split by a crude ax; some are ornate with the carving of gnomes and goblins, peering with a leer or sneer from some crevice or corner; and high on the hillside is the home of the cow girl tending invisible herds in the green valley below.

All this would count for little, however, were it not for nature's setting. Fed by innumerable springs, a sparkling trout brook winds through the twisting gulch, finally uniting with other creeks and streams to pour its waters into the historic Wisconsin. Sheltered by wooded ridges[27] it is an enthralling scene in spring to watch the sunlight peer over the crest and then swiftly flood the verdant valley with golden light. The morning air clean with the smell of fresh earth and early flowers is exhilarating. I confess a certain juvenile exaltation to find here the mountain recesses of Old Norway so vividly pictured in my childhood dreams. The sheer physical beauty of this country never ceases to captivate me.

Perhaps by noontime the dream may become an actuality. For often kindred groups come here to spend the day in picnics and to sing their Norwegian songs. Sometimes folklore societies, as far away as Chicago, arrive dressed in native costumes. Then the dance tunes of Old Norway echo over the hills. And around in shade and sun are fleeting glimpses of golden-haired children with faces as pink as ripening apples.

The Norwegian Lutheran church has done much to keep alive this love of traditions and characteristics of the mother country. Many of the sermons are still preached in the mother tongue, and children are taught to speak the language and sing the old songs with a fervor and respect not always similarly cherished among the youth of other transplanted nationalities. The Norwegian has a pride in nationality.

Church societies have made the "lutefisk dinner," held in the Norwegian settlements in early fall, a community institution. Hundreds of barrels of lutefisk loaded on Norwegian steamers, heading out of the fjords for Wisconsin are an annual item of trade — at this writing restricted by the second World War. Lutefisk is a long, cod, carp-like fish caught in the North Sea, along the coast of Norway. It is split into "sides" and taken to the mountains to dry.

"There is nothing like the Norwegian mountain air to cure a fish," vowed Oscar Hippi, chef at the East Koshkonong church lutefisk dinner, where 1,200 pounds of fish are required to feed the hundreds who come miles for the annual event.[28] "That's why they can't prepare it in this country; the climate's wrong."

When the fish has been dried to the consistency of a pine board by the long days of the northern summer sun, it is ready for crating and shipment. To prepare for the table requires several days of softening in lye water and then a prolonged bath in a salt solution. The Norwegian cook knows, better than any other, the exact time to remove the fish from the brine at the point of the highest flavor. Great hunks of the flaky fish, when cooked, are served like boiled cabbage at the supper.

But lutefisk is only a part of the feast. Meat balls (Kaoppboller), new potatoes, huge bowls of pickled beets and creamed cabbage; lefse and flatbrod for breads; rice pudding (risetro grot) and cream pudding (flotegrot) for dessert; great cups of steaming coffee and many kinds of ordinary pies and cookies are items in the meal. The lutefisk is served with a melted butter sauce; the lefse comes in circular sheets to be buttered, sprinkled with sugar, rolled, and then eaten like a lollipop; the kitchen workers, men and women, are organized like a circus crew expeditiously to feed the hungry, who sometimes must wait patiently for hours to be served but with never a grumble.

For years I have attended lutefisk suppers. At first I could eat only sparingly, but after a time I, too, came to relish the food. If there is a Norwegian church in the settlements that does not hold such a gathering annually, I have not learned of it. From October 15 to Christmas one who dined publicly on lutefisk meals would not go hungry. One dealer at Stoughton sells an average of five tons of lutefisk annually; a Viroqua merchant has a regular sale for one church dinner of four hundred pounds. Vernon County residents consume twenty-five tons in an ordinary normal year. It has been estimated that over fifty tons of this imported fish are consumed annually in Wisconsin.

There are some characteristics among the Norwegians that appear inconsistent. They vote dry on referendums and in the legislature, but a goodly number of individual members drink. Gathered convivially around the bar they toast fellows with the "Skoal" for good health. Some men of prominence have broken away from their old religious moorings, but when they come to die, it is not uncommon to hold for them a double funeral service — one in the English language and one in Norwegian. [29] In the care of their orphans and the aged, they do not follow the usual American pattern of making their unfortunates wards of the state. Rather, they continue the Old World ideal of the Catholics and the Lutherans of founding their own separate institutions. The Martin Luther Children's Home and the Skaalen Sunset Home, both near Stoughton, and the only "Home for Aged Indians" at Wittenberg, are all under Norwegian Lutheran church guidance.

Lawyers who practice in Norwegian-settled communities soon learn how to draw one legal document peculiar to the people — the "Norwegian deed." By this instrument the son or daughter purchasing the home acres agrees to support and maintain the parents and give them a Christian burial. An examination of the

Wisconsin Reports indicates, however, that this form of document is used in other than Norwegian localities. It has been uniformly upheld by the Supreme Court in protecting the rights and interests of the parents[30] Perhaps this form of conveyance accounts for the continuance of ownership in one family often found in many Old World communities in Wisconsin.

Even during a short tour of the Vernon County Norwegian settlement one comes to understand two factors in the life of the people — the land and heredity. Something in the fertility of the soil in this rolling, unglaciated section has made it the richest tobacco section of the state. To look upon the big tobacco warehouses at Viroqua and Westby is to realize anew that wealth comes from the farms. It is a pleasant ride in the sunlit hills and valleys.

To talk to the people is to gain an insight into racial solidarity. Ever since the town of Westby was founded, the mayor, the village manager, and the town chairman have been Norwegians. There is much rivalry between Westby and Viroqua on the athletic field and the basketball courts. One of the yells that is given by opponents of Westby goes something like this:

"Lutefisk, Lutefisk, Yah! Yah! Yah! — Westby High School, Bah! Bah! Bah!" There is a bowling team of young women employed in Viroqua that has typical Norwegian costumes which they wear when they bowl. They go under the sobriquet of "Vikings." The names on professional cards and business places in both Westby and Viroqua have an Old World ring if properly inflected when pronounced; most of the people met on their streets are blond of hair and complexion, a Norwegian characteristic.

The Norwegian race in general is a strong, virile one, with strong, well-proportioned men. This is believed due in part to the fact that as Norway has had no wars practically for a thousand years the able-bodied men were not killed off and the race was not perpetuated by the smaller, weaker, more defective men.

Likewise, as Norway has had no military power to be feared, and has had no ambitions of conquest, people of Norse blood in

America and elsewhere have never been feared nor suspected. Such nationality customs and practices as they have observed in the transitional period of Americanization have been preserved for sentimental and cultural reasons and not for ulterior dreams and national aspirations. It is said that no foreign, non-English-speaking people has fallen into the American spirit and way of living and thinking so quickly and completely as has the Norwegian.

It was probably because of this fine physique, coupled with an innate sense of duty to give service for pay, that the Norwegian immigrants made such excellent farm hands in the '60s, '70s and '80s, the period of great agricultural expansion in the Northwest. Nearly every young Norwegian immigrant had to begin as a hired man. Many of them were frightfully exploited by their employers and bore a role worthy the name of Trojan. Working days were often — pretty generally — from 4 a.m. to 10 o'clock at night. And coming from a colder climate, and often wearing heavier clothing unsuited to the hot American summers, these farm laborers often suffered terribly in the long days of driving toil. Yet they were strong to endure and regarded the conditions imposed upon them as necessary to their final winning of a place in America. Through frugality and industry they were able in most cases soon to establish themselves as owners of farms of their own and in time as independent citizens of the republic which they loved so much.

There is a deep blueness in their eyes that seems to vision distant horizons; a reserve and caution of speech characteristic of the loneliness of ancient fjord and mountain.

These are the people who became the virile political backbone of the Progressive movement in Wisconsin. Their loyalty of support has largely directed many of the moral and social trends of the state.

[24] Barton, Albert O. and Haugen, Einar, **Norwegians in the Life of Wisconsin,** souvenir brochure issued on the occasion of the visit to Madison of Crown Prince Olav and Crown Princess Martha, June 19-20, 1939; Ronning, N. N., **The Saga of Old Muskego,** St. Paul, 1943.

[25] Schafer. Joseph, **Scandinavian Moravians in Wisconsin,** Wisconsin Magazine of History, Madison, September, 1940, pp. 25-38.

[26] St. Paul Sunday Pioneer Press, June 7, 1925, **Norse-American Centennial,** Seventh Section; Colbo, Ella Stratton. **Historic Heg Memorial Park** Racine, 1940, pp. 37-39; Ylvisaker, Erling, Eminent Pioneers, Minneapolis 1934, pp. 81-93. A bronze statue of Col Hans Heg, who fell in the battle of Chickamauga, Sept. 19, 1863, has been erected in the Capitol Park at Madison, and replicas have been unveiled at Muskego, his American home, and at Lier, his Norwegian birthplace.

[27] Cave of the Mounds, annually visited by many thousands opened in 1940 in one of these extended hillsides about a mile from "Little Norway." It is a subterranean wonderland on whose walls and needlelike formations are written a fascinating story of earth sculpturing. Described by author in The Capital Times, Madison, Wis., June 23, 1940.

[28] For detailed description of event and methods of cooking, see Wisconsin State Journal, Madison, Wis., Nov. 10, 1940.

[29] Wisconsin Magazine of History, Vol. XIV, p. 430.

[30] **Wanner vs. Wanner,** 115 Wisconsin, 196. **Yates vs. Weinhardt,** 224 Wisconsin, 496.

❖

CHAPTER VI

Holland's Puritan Ways
Oostburg and Cedar Grove

A LONE man strolled toward the outskirts of Oostburg, his white hair protruding unevenly from beneath his dark woolen cap, his pipe hanging loosely in his jaws. As he leisurely approached, I waited beside my car. Occasionally he would stop at a cross walk to look down the street at the long line of parked automobiles; then he would pause to view a tree bursting into leaf or a flower bed breaking into bloom.

"They're all in church," he remarked, as he met my wondering eyes and was about to pass when I engaged him in conversation.

"Nothing but church here on Sundays," he continued. "Four of them are now going on. No other places are open. When the religious services are over, these streets will be deserted in a few moments. Subscribers to Sunday papers will get them tomorrow. This is a day of rest."

Nearly fifteen miles south of Sheboygan, gathered about Oostburg and Cedar Grove, is the largest center of Hollanders in Wisconsin. Their ancestors came seeking a haven for religious freedom. And they found it in this countryside tempered by the restless winds of Lake Michigan, as if bringing again from the land of dykes the bracing air of the ocean. They cherished in their hearts longings that were soon to kindle the imagination of all Europe and stir life in all America.

Discouragements recurring from the repeated inundation of the Rhine bottomlands by the Atlantic and dissension and opposition arising over announced religious tenets stirred an otherwise stolid people to emigrate. Hope beckoned from the Wisconsin horizon. Two or three Dutch families came to

Sheboygan County as early as 1844, but members of the two nearby early settlements — Amsterdam and Oostburg — did not embark until 1847. The first, coming under the direction of their pastor, Reverend Peter Zonne, by way of the Hudson River, Erie Canal and the Great Lakes, colonized on Lake Michigan shore lands, entered from the government domain the year before in anticipation of their arrival.[31] The second group settled inland two miles north, at East Oostburg, now an almost forgotten hamlet.

Soon the countryside was called Holland Town, a designation appropriately adopted for the subdivision by the county government. It was close to the ever-changing, threatening lake waters that the Hollanders founded a community, which they named Amsterdam, after the thriving Dutch capital of the homeland. Later, this site was abandoned for an inland location, but the new community had already been designated as Cedar Grove, because of the dark, encircling evergreen forests, now only a memory. With the coming of the railroad in 1872, Oostburg, the other nearby community of Hollanders, also moved further inland and the present village sprang into existence around the flour mill of Peter Daane. Soon he achieved a political leadership among his countrymen akin to that exercised in the religious field by the Rev. Mr. Zonne.

Even in colonial days, Dutch fur traders in New York were interested in Wisconsin. There was an early Holland beginning in Green Bay, where a neglected wind grist mill of stone still stands as a landmark of the period. Permanent settlements were not made until the pre-statehood period.[32] A considerable Dutch community of Catholics was established in 1844 at Little Chute in Outagamie County and in the surrounding country under the guidance of Father T. J. Van den Broek, and scattered Protestant neighborhood groups gathered early around Waupun. A large migration of Friesians arrived by the New Orleans-Mississippi River route in 1853 after the terrifying experience of a shipwreck in the West Indies and founded Holland township and the village of New Amsterdam, north of La Crosse. Glimpsing the prospect of possible pastoral scenes common to the Netherlands, they selected a low and level stretch of Mississippi bottomlands. This is in contrast to the Swiss who came about the same period to this section but settled further north at Fountain City and Alma, building their homes on the steep sides of bluffs. Like the Oostburg settlers, the La Crosse Holland community has become recognized for its fine dairy herds and advanced dairy activities. Likewise, near Barton in Washington County and at Alto in Fond du Lac County are communities that continue essentially Dutch.

Pronounced differences over religion, the threat of the free exercise of which helped to stimulate the trek from the Old World, still persist in the Holland settlements of Wisconsin. Oostburg, with a population under eight hundred, supports four prosperous Protestant churches — First Reformed, Christian Reformed, often called the "Immigrant Church," First Presbyterian and Orthodox Presbyterian. In addition, three of these denominations have churches at Cedar Grove.

Strict adherence to Calvinistic doctrines by the Sheboygan County Hollanders and the partial retention of the Dutch language in religious services have nurtured and preserved ideals and usages to a degree not to be found in the other Wisconsin Dutch transplantations. Their foreign ways are not as pronounced as those observed on my visits among the Hollanders at Pella, Iowa, where Dutch customs are a colorful part of the annual tulip festival.[33] But they are sufficiently different to give them a place among Wisconsin's foreign groups.

Almost at the outset of my tour of the Sheboygan settlement, I came to the community cemetery.[34] Seized with a desire to see the graves of the pioneers, I was about to enter the gate when I saw this sign:

HOLLAND SETTLEMENT

Settlers came to this vicinity in 1846 under the leadership of G. H. Te Kolste. Just north of here in 1847 the steamboat "Phoenix" with many new recruits to this colony was burned. 127 Hollanders were lost in this disaster.

If the cryptic story of the tragedy was to awaken my deep sympathy for the trials of the early Hollanders, other visits several weeks later to the abandoned home sites of the two pioneer settlements were to remind me that all through the intervening years these people have been moving forward along pathways destiny seems to have charted for them centuries ago. In the great gallery of Wisconsin's nationalities, they are the prototypes of men whose faith, fearlessness and frugality seldom change.

Watching the fishermen haul in their heavy nets along the naked beach of the Lake Michigan shore required some vision to picture Amsterdam as it was in the early days. Perhaps under those spreading evergreen trees, the first Hollanders smoked their pipes as they searched the grey scene of billowing waters for a ship's spar that might be the signal of tidings of friends from the homeland. But in most roseate dreams they could not have divined the day when the densely wooded countryside would give way to modern dairyland activities.

Rich soil and not rare scenery was to guide the final selection of their homesites. Today Amsterdam is a ghost town with only the dilapidated red school house, a rendezvous for bats, still standing. Shifting sands have buried all traces of roads and townsite. Nature pays but little attention to the works of the past. With the quiet of evening, only moving waters lift their voices to chant a requiem for the departed. East Oostburg fares little better. A few buildings have crowded close to the highway as if in a last stand against an invader. But with my discovery of the removal of the first churches to Oostburg, I had a sad feeling that the spirit of the historic days had almost vanished.

That was a transitory thought to be routed from mind by a roadside sight that flashed suddenly before me a few minutes later. In the yard a man was sharpening posts for the building of a fence. One glance and I saw that for which I was searching. With a jerk I wheeled the automobile through the farm gate. Here was a Hollander wearing wooden shoes.

From him I was to learn that the wearing of wooden shoes is more comfortable in the winter when heavy, hand-knitted woolen socks fill snugly the foot opening.

"Not so many wear them regularly now," he explained. "But if you will examine the back porch of almost any farm home you will find a well worn pair. There are times when it is mighty convenient to slip them on. They are still sold in the stores at Oostburg."

"Where are they made?" I inquired.

"Over at Gibbsville is a maker of wooden shoes. He is the only cobbler of wood left in the community."

William Ros is one of the most approachable men I have ever met. He was returning from work in his apiary as I arrived at his farm. When he learned of the purpose of my visit, he took me into the shop where every winter he fashions from sixty to seventy pairs of wooden shoes to supply the local demand. When I complimented him on the fine craftsmanship of his work, he told me that he had learned the trade in Holland over fifty years ago. Piled high to the woodshed door were blocks that looked like wood lengths sawed for a fireplace. These he used in shoe manufacturing.

"Come out under the shade, where I have a shoe bench and some of my tools and I will show you how it is done," continued the white haired shoemaker as he led the way.

A long knife was employed to pare the block down. Notches in the tabletop helped to hold the piece of wood in place during the shaping process. From a kit of chisels he made selections, employing them to hollow out the foot part.

"Only bass wood is used," he explained as he bent to the task. "It is soft and yields easily to sharp tools. The most difficult part is the gouging out of the place for the toes."

"Are wooden shoes expensive?"

"From a dollar down, depending on the size. One pair will last several years."

"Do some prefer them to leather shoes?"

"They are fine to wear while doing chores in winter. If a cow steps on your toe it doesn't hurt. Afterward, when you come in from the barn, it's easy to kick them off and go about the house in stocking feet."

Several pairs of old wooden shoes were piled in a corner of the woodshed. I stopped to examine them. Two were carefully inlaid with barnyard straw to take the place of insoles.

"Wooden shoes never leak water," advised the shoemaker as he resumed his carving. "And if you learn how, they are as easy to dance in as slippers."

And as he spoke there came to mind scenes of tulip festivals at Pella, Iowa, and Holland, Michigan, where wooden shoe dances are events in which the whole countryside participates. There is a rhythm in it not apparent in the other less classical dances.

Returning to Oostburg by a short route, I passed the Gibbsville grist mill, still driven by the pent up waters of the Onion River. To it, early Hollanders and their neighbors carried on their backs wheat to be made into flour. Standing at the flume, I watched the fretted waters that turn the turbines go swishing through the strainers. But as I looked up to scan the peaceful farm landscape, green with spring crops, I thought how strange it was in this world of so many changes that one of the first businesses established in the neighborhood should still be flourishing. Every sizeable stream with sufficient waterfall was harnessed by the first settlers to furnish power for early industries. The first millers were men of skill; they had to work long hours; they took their wages in toll from the grindings. In the life of the community they were a vital factor. Oftentimes farmers would travel fifty miles and stand in line for hours to have their grinding done. And yet the pioneer miller has found neither troubadour nor historian to sing his praise. If I could learn the name of the first Hollander who operated this grist mill I would perpetuate it in these pages.

Entering the Oostburg State Bank, I met President John Brethower, a Hollander, and asked him where I might find the tulip beds for which most Dutch communities are distinctive.

"They are not here, the temperatures on this side of Lake Michigan are different from the east shore," he told me. "Attempts have been made to grow them but a sudden drop in the thermometer ruins the blossoms. This atmospheric vagary accounts for the intensive cultivation across the lake at Holland, Michigan, and the total lack of their appearance here."

Answering questions regarding the character of these people, he said that local insurance records disclose the Hollanders enjoy a high moral reputation as a fire insurance risk. He couldn't recall a single case of arson in the community history. Agents give this as the reason for the low community rates.

"The record of the Hollanders in matters of credit is good." And then, he added, ironically, "It hasn't improved any since the great European war."

As it was approaching noon I anticipated eagerly the opportunity to eat kaffie kletz, babbelbar, and other Holland foods. Keutje is the most popular of all their dishes. It is a vegetable dinner, made principally of pork, potatoes and cabbage. Dutch housewives attribute its appetizing taste to the fact that "the vegetables are cooked through each other." Coffee is a staple drink at meals, and on the farms in summer the workers are served a light lunch of coffee and doughnuts in the morning at 10 o'clock and in the afternoon at 3 o'clock. At special family gatherings suiker speks is served. This is a boiled candy made of brown sugar, syrup, butter, and a dash of vinegar. Not many members of the younger generation can make it, although they prefer it to chocolate fudge. Saturday is bake day for the Dutch housewives. Only the most necessary cooking is done on Sundays.

Despite the dreary efforts of modern civilization to enforce conformity on all peoples, it has not succeeded here. About fifty percent of the inhabitants in the Sheboygan County Holland community can speak the Dutch language. It is used in the afternoon Sunday sermons and sung in church hymns. The Wilhelmus Van Nassause, a stirring sixteenth century national air of the Netherlands, is played by the high school band on patriotic occasions.

The two older churches — First Reformed and Christian Reformed — are within the business district in Oostburg. Their type of architecture gives a foreign appearance that is particularly intriguing. Up until a few years ago Cedar Grove had in addition an academy offering classical courses to those desiring to enter the ministry. This has been abandoned.

"How can these small communities support several denominations?" I asked one of the merchants.

"Hollanders are stubborn about their beliefs," was the answer. "They gladly pay the price of religious freedom."

Dutch weddings are pretty church affairs. Sometimes the whole congregation turns out to honor the young couple. It is a distinctive religious ceremony often followed by a sermon. Church and school play cooperative community roles. Because neither dance halls nor movies are permitted in the community, special entertainment by school and church seem to cement community interests. Children grow up to know their own parents and to respect their counsel.

Annually, in June, Holland Town in Southwestern Brown County celebrates "Schut" Sunday. It is a semi-religious civic event that tests the skill of marksmanship. It is a traditional Dutch custom brought to this country by the early settlers nearly a century ago.

Admission to the "Schut" is accorded only to those who comply with certain Catholic church requirements and conform to definite rules of sportsmanship. Every son is a hereditary member upon reaching his twenty-first birthday, and the boys look forward to participation in the shooting adventure with as much interest as if it were akin to admission into the knighthood of royalty. The winner becomes "King" of the "Schut" for the year, entitled to don the scarlet coat that has been worn by every king since 1848, and to have a medal cast from spent bullets to be worn and to have his record preserved in the archives of the order.[35]

The shooting grounds are owned by the St. Francis Society, which operates it independent of church affairs. It is a three-acre plot on a little ridge about a quarter of a mile from the hamlet's buildings. In the center of the arena is a sectional eighty-foot pole. A wooden bird fashioned from the root of an elm tree, with a wing spread of about thirty inches, is bolted securely to the top. Riflemen try to hit the bird, and the one who shoots away the last bit of the wooden figure is declared "King" of the "Schut" for the ensuing year.

Elaborate ceremonials, emulous of the dignity and spiritual traditions that brought the "Schut" into existence in Holland many centuries ago, are followed. The "Schut" opens with mass at St. Francis Church at which the members receive holy communion in a body. Afterwards they gather at Van Abel's hall, where the society's treasures are kept on display, and march, some wearing wooden shoes, to the grounds.

Before the shooting is begun there is music followed by prayers for all deceased members of the society. Then the forty or more men form a circle around the pole, with their deer rifles all primed. The bird which is provided by the king of the last "Schut" is elevated and the pastor traditionally fires the first shot. Because the king for 1941 was called into military service his "queen" was allowed to shoot, the only woman to be accorded this privilege. Shooting is done in rotation.

"It requires from 470 to 700 shots to win," explained Rev. Cornelius Raymakers. "Afterwards the day is given to feasting and celebrations. The 'Schut' is the permanent link connecting the past with the present. At the centenary of the 'St. Francis Schut' in 1949 it is planned to erect a monument worthy of such skilled marksmen and fathers by the then living members. This will instill in the minds of the coming generations the adventurous will of those who subdued this wilderness section of Wisconsin."

With a glow of anticipation, I entered the hall where the mementoes are kept. The medals are preserved in a case beside which stands a Holland clock that has ticked away the decades since 1722. It seemed extraordinary that the quaint past should come so close to me. But so it seemed, however, and I lingered there a long time, visiting with men who only yesterday were heroes in action.

And so there comes a satisfaction in learning that there are communities in Wisconsin where the old ways are not entirely forgotten, where whole-souled religious devotion is not passé, where an epitome of Holland history and scenery will repay more than a passing glance from an automobile, and where the visitor may depart with joyous memories to brighten the long nights of coming winter.

---

[31] Rederus, Sipke F., **The Dutch Settlement of Sheboygan County**, Wisconsin Magazine of History, Vol. I, p. 256; Ibid, Vol. II, pp. 464-466, and Vol. XI, p. 234.

[32] Information gained through personal interviews at Oostburg in the Summer of 1941, with John Brethouwer, Arnold Tre Ronde John Ten Dollen, W. Henry Bruggink, and others. For Green Bay and Fox River Valley settlement, see Alphonsa, Sister Mary, The Story of Father Van den Broek, Chicago (1907), and Proceedings, State Historical Society of Wisconsin, Vol. XXXVII, p. 61: for La Crosse County settlement, see La Crosse Tribune, April 24, 19Zl. and October 7. 1924.

[33] Adamic, Louis, **From Foreign Lands**, p. 165, et seq., gives a description of this Iowa settlement.

[34] On U. S. Highway 41 about two miles southeast of Oostburg and near the present East Oostburg, the original Holland settlement of that name; Havighurst, Walter, **The Long Ships Passing**, New York, 1942, pp. 132-133.

[35] Holland Town is on County Trunk Q, seven miles east of Little Chute. St. Francis Catholic church is the landmark of the settlement. Data on the Fox River Valley settlement and "Schut" customs were gathered in an interview with Rev. Cornelius Raymakers, Pastor. The meet is held annually on the Sunday following the second Tuesday in June.

❖

CHAPTER VII

Swiss Yodel Cares Away
New Glarus

GESSLER: I do not want your life, Tell . . .

WALTER: Come, Father, shoot!

EDWARD VOLLENWEIDER, a New Glarus farmer, impersonating Wilhelm Tell, nervously adjusted his crossbow and aimed the arrow at the apple on the head of the boy. Not a muscle in the breathless audience of 5,000 moved. The silence of the rural countryside seemed suspended for the moment.

There was a flash of light!

"The apple is down," shouted a worker and in that split second the spell was broken by a woman's piercing cry:

"The boy's alive."

At Elmer's Grove in a natural amphitheater that commands a sloping hillside set with trees at the outskirts of New Glarus, descendants from the cantons of far away Switzerland re-enact every autumn, in color and gallantry, Schiller's pageant-drama, "Wilhelm Tell." It is the story of Switzerland's famous peasant, the ever-moving cry of man's struggle for freedom. On one day 200 country folk present the play in German and on the day following in English. Students from the German department of the University of Wisconsin and "Schweitzers" from the settlements in Milwaukee and in the Upper Mississippi Valley, tourists and townspeople, all sit captivated by the rural actors in atmospheric Old World surroundings as for nearly three hours they give voice to a tremendous drama of heroic literature. In those two days at least the new is crowded out and the glamour of the past recalled with all its deathless glory.

Wilhelm Tell is the mythical hero of the Swiss people. Shooting gallery and hotel, tavern and community guild bear his name in New Glarus. He is said to have belonged to the canton of Uri and to have enlisted the support of other communities in resisting the Austrians. On his refusal to do homage to Gessler's hat, set on a pole, he was seized and condemned to death, but gained his freedom by a remarkable feat of marksmanship. Theme and scene have since become companions in thought for homesick Swiss in seasons of adversity.

I was one who sat enraptured as the old drama unfolded in the valley before me. The voices of the players scarcely had died away when over the hills came the sweet tinkle of Swiss bells and the lowing of uneasy cows awaiting the delayed milking. The man who sat beside me during the performance now turned to remark that because of the tons of milk produced in Green County each day, this section stands first in the state for individual farm income. Suddenly my mind came back to the scenes of the morning, to the herds of Holstein and Brown Swiss in sunny pastures and to the big red barns with Gothic hay ventilators and south side wooden shelter canopies to protect the cattle from wind and bad weather. Someone described this rugged land as "Swissylvania," and the slogan stuck.

New Glarus is one of the most fascinating of the Old World towns in Wisconsin. Unlike the others, it had its beginning as a foreign government project. It is one of those places that hold you by a charm all its own. I have come to believe that it is the exaltation in reminiscing about heroic events through the centuries that gives to it this mystical atmosphere. Fifty years ago it was predicted that a hundred years would merge the identity of these transplanted people. It now seems doubtful whether a thousand years could accomplish that result. Instead, there are evidences that the customs of industry and thrift, work and play, are being gradually acquired by neighboring communities.

Some impulse prompted me to stop near the crest of the

twisting hill road that runs into New Glarus from the North. Before me lay the valley of the Little Sugar River and a sweep of undulating farm country, where were experienced many of the sorrows and triumphs of these immigrants. The shadow of a torn cloud moved across the scene, trailed by a burst of sunshine, as if retracing for me in graphic form the pathway of the settler's deliverance.

When opportunities for employment diminished in Switzerland because of an increasing population, and the food supply decreased because of a consequent smaller redivision of use in the public lands, national leaders sought means to relieve the distress. Then, in 1844, came an almost complete crop failure. At long last, stories of the vast land acreages being opened in the Mississippi Valley of the United States offered a possible solution. At government expense two agents were sent to America to locate a tract for a colony. While they viewed possible sites in Illinois, Missouri, Iowa and Wisconsin, so swiftly did plans move in Switzerland that the one hundred ninety-three persons of all ages and both sexes to make the settlement started at once on their journey.[36]

Finally, the advance agents were shown lands in the Sugar Valley of Southern Wisconsin. The ruggedness of the hills and valleys, the presence of running water and wild game reminded them of the home country. Entry was made July 17, 1845, at Mineral Point, covering a single tract of 1,200 acres. Within a month, after many delays and disappointments, the one hundred and eight of the once hopeful band of immigrants who remained came trekking across the wilderness country of Southern Wisconsin from Galena. Carrying their pots, pans, kettles and other utensils, these poverty-stricken foreigners arrived in their land of promise, August 15, 1845. One feels the wisdom of the choice of this spot, surrounded by valleys that are rounded and beautifully shaped.

According to adopted plans, land was divided among the heads of the families. For a time all were housed in one hut, as narrow and humble as the birthplace of Abraham Lincoln. Before Christmas other cabins were finished and the newcomers settled down to await springtime and planting. The hardships of the next twenty years could never have been overcome had it not been for the Christian forbearance of individual members. Yet these people lived joyously. A group of pioneer cabins that stand today as a memorial in one of the public parks is a visual historical testimonial of the poverty, privations and penury of those times. A Swiss chalet of grace and beauty recently erected on a site overlooking the village must have been like a vision that kept them contented and hopeful. Brawn won this inevitable battle.

Their early fate was not too long delayed. During the spring of 1846 drovers from Ohio brought a herd of cows to Exeter, a mining hamlet less than ten miles away. Long trained in the raising of livestock, this was an opportunity. A sufficient number of the best animals were selected to give each family a cow. Payments of $12.00 a head were made out of balances in the subsistence fund created by the Swiss government to found the settlement. It was quite natural that the colonists should again make the saucer-like cheeses to which they had been accustomed back home.

Out of this fortuitous start has grown the great foreign cheese industry that has given to Wisconsin first rank in the nation for the production of Swiss and Limburger cheese. New lands were acquired, factories were built, and eventually cheese-making displaced wheat-raising. The tiller became a herdsman. Trained cheese-makers were brought from the valley of the Emmen; rennet, copper kettles, tools and supplies were imported from Switzerland; the district crossed county lines and extended north to Dane and west into Iowa and Lafayette. Prosperity arrived and the Swiss government debt created by the founders was discharged.

Ultimately the cooperative factory system was adopted. Democracy was introduced into the cheese business. Now the farmers hire a cheese-maker for the neighborhood and sell the product monthly to wholesalers at Monroe, eighteen miles to the south, which has grown commercially as to be styled "Swiss Cheese Capital of the United States." All this seems simple in the telling. But for the colonists the way was beset with trials innumerable.

Every morning the country roads in "Little Switzerland" are a procession of milk trucks. The making of Swiss cheese is an exact science. It requires about 3,000 pounds of milk to make one of those big 220-pound cartwheels. Five to eight weeks' ripening is necessary to turn out the best product. The eye formation in the cheese is controlled by the maker, who develops his own prime culture of bacteria to produce the big holes in the cheese.

"Much like yeast causes bread dough to rise, bacteria in the pressed curd of a big Swiss cheese get in their good work while the cheese is on the shelves in the warm curing room," explained Emery A. Odell, the editor of the only daily paper in the district, as he took me through a Monroe plant.

"The carbon dioxide produced by these organisms gradually accumulates to cause bubbles in the 'meat' of the cheese, slowly expanding the big wheel until its sides bulge slightly and it is said to have 'opened up.' The organisms not only cause bubbles, which are the 'eyes' when the big cheese is cut, but they also help produce the pleasant hazelnut flavor characteristic of Swiss cheese."

Amazed over the development and financial importance of the industry, I consulted a report of the Wisconsin Department of Agriculture found on the desk of the manager of the largest wholesale cheese agency. The cattle census in the Swiss district outnumbers the district's population three to one; there is an average of 27 cows on every farm, and 95 percent of the farmers are engaged in dairying. Cows on Green County farms annually produce 270,000,000 pounds of milk per year. If this sea of milk were pumped through the water mains of Madison, it would require four days to exhaust the supply at the average rate water is consumed in Wisconsin's capital city.

"Since the farmers of the Swiss district produce so much profitably marketed milk, how do you explain the community's high farm mortgage ratio?" a New Glarus banker was asked.

"Two factors contribute," was the answer. "The Swiss have

better farm plants than elsewhere in the state. Look at their barns and homes and compare them with the low mortgage districts. Then again, in the past ten years, there has been a big shift of ownership from father to son, necessitating large credit. The Swiss farmer is a business man and he knows what he is doing. There is nothing alarming in the fact that Green County has the second highest farm mortgage rate in the state. It means only that the Swiss farmers need credit to operate and to expand."

If great numbers of farmers while herding their stock or milking their cows in the evening yodel the cares of the day; if an occasional farmer with a longing for Alpine landscape has had a boyhood scene from Switzerland painted on the side of his barn; if still others exhibit pride in big cone-shaped woodpiles that look like ancient beehives, reminiscent of the Bernese highlands; if barns seem to rival each other, it is but the Old Swiss instinct of joyousness, thrift and industry outwardly manifesting itself.

Swiss ideals of democracy permeate New Glarus' civic life. The "thrifty Swiss" have declined every Works Progress Administration project offered during the seven years that the Federal Government had aided towns, villages and cities in the United States. All municipal work is performed by village residents, and relief costs are reduced by furnishing work to men who otherwise might find it necessary to ask for aid. As an evidence of economy, the New Glarus tax rate is the second lowest in Wisconsin, and Green County for the sixth successive year (1941) had the lowest percentage of real estate tax levy sold at delinquent tax sales of all Wisconsin counties. Citizens of Swiss descent pay strict attention to the character of the officials they select in order not to repent later, as in some other communities for the manner in which officers have mismanaged public affairs.

The Swiss farmer is a stocky fellow interested in dairying and church, but with a heart as light as the bobolink that sings over his alfalfa fields.

I found myself, as every visitor does, irresistibly caught by the yodeling of the Swiss farmers. For years I have planned my summer routes so that I might be out in the heart of the farming district at milking time. Just stop the automobile and wait. Hark to the soaring of some of the melodious words!

Uf de Bargenisch guet labe
d'Ehuejer jutze nit vergabe!

Hie, wonus d'Fluchlerche singe, hie wo d'Gemscheni
Oldi vor is springe, wie de Vogel i de Lufte isch hie

Ho-li-di o ho-li-o u-i-du-li
Ho-li-di hol-di-o
Ho u-i-du hol-di-o

Yodeling is not confined to the farms. Occasionally a yodeler will pipe up in a tavern to entertain his friends. Quickly a crowd will assemble. Singing societies are the rule in the Swiss district. Every gathering place has a well thumbed yodel book.[37] New Glarus has a Mannerchor of over sixty voices that meets regularly. Two organizations of yodelers dressed in native garb make annual tours of the state. The Turner Hall at Monroe is a central gathering place for both singers and yodelers.

This is not strange, since about fifty percent of the people of Green County and over ninety percent in New Glarus village are of Swiss descent. Postal authorities estimate that ten percent of them keep up a correspondence with relatives in Switzerland, and that fifty percent converse naturally in the Swiss dialect. Money is still sent to aid relatives in the old country. Skiing and wrestling are hereditary sports that enlist the interest of the young men.

With the hard work of the summer drawing to a close, the Wisconsin Swiss become more festive. Swiss Day, commemorating the national independence of the home country, is celebrated the first Sunday in August, followed by the Wilhelm Tell drama on the last Saturday and Sunday at the end of the month.

Services in German are held in the churches on alternate Sundays. The hymnals used bear the imprint of a Swiss publisher. Around the Evangelical and Reformed Church, to which most of the Swiss churchgoers belong, rotates the community life. Placed on a hill in the center of the village, its spire is discernible from all directions. It is a red brick structure, with beautiful Gothic windows. In the yard are the time-worn tombstones of some of the founders, including that of Nicholas Duerst, the adviser, who kept the colony going during the early troublesome years. There is also an Evangelical Church in the community.

All holidays blend in the Kibli, a church anniversary conducted by the Reformed Congregation on the last Sunday of each September. At the close of the regular services the church building is rededicated. During the afternoon target shooting, hornus set, an Old World form of ball game, and dancing are moderately indulged in.

And in the homes there is feasting. Fresh bread and butter are served especially. Honey is accorded a prominent place at these festivities. The food that is best known and served most often is kalberwurst, a calf sausage made of veal, pork, crackers and milk and cooked in ways seemingly known only to the Swiss housewife.

"This dish alone is worth coming miles to eat," Dr. E. D. McQuillin, mayor of New Glarus, advised me. "When with it you are served the regular vegetables together with pear bread and cookies with the familiar Swiss ring to them — Schweitzer bretli, springerle, lebkuchen and pfefernuss — you will have had a meal fit for royalty."

"Where can one be served such a meal?" I interrupted.

"Across the valley, at the farm home of Mrs. Esther Stauffacher . . ."

A Swiss meal—and kalberwurst! How shall I ever tell the story? Maybe I can recall the tempting conversation as Mrs. Stauffacher served the delicious food.[38]

"This is 'pfafa klotz' . . . potatoes cut in chunks, buttered and mixed up with cream sauce to which parsley and onion grass (chives) have been added for garnish. These 'fissels' (whole green beans) are prepared with the same sauce, without the onion grass."

"Zoklas," she said to our interrogatory glance at a large bowl of what looked like scrambled eggs. "A sort of dumpling made out of egg, milk, water, flour and salt, dropped in boiling chicken gravy, then drained and fried in butter. Sprinkle some of this 'ziger' over them.

" 'Ziger' . . . that's green cheese, made of alpine herbs and whey. This lettuce 'salat' is fresh garden lettuce served with Swiss sour cream dressing. Try some of this dried fruit conserve. It's in your 'zuri beter' . . . your dessert, too. That's pie crust rolled with dried fruit as a filling, and whipped cream on top.

"Here are two breads . . . an egg bread braid and hot butter rolls. And, of course, you recognize this as Swiss cheese. Now, fall to before it all gets cold."

Afterward I was to discover that several of these foods could be purchased at the local meat market, bakery, or grocery store. But I still knew that it was the method of cooking and serving that gave them the appetizing taste.

It was with regret that I found one well-known church custom had been recently discontinued. Like a legend it lingers in community traditions. For three-quarters of a century after the settlement it was the custom for the female members of the congregation to leave the church first while the bell in the steeple was being rung and the men remained standing. Then would follow the male members of the congregation followed by their pastor. This was done in deference to the memory of an attempted ambush of the members at church in the town of Nafels, in old Glarus, by the Austrians some five hundred years ago. Discovery of the enemy's ruse was made by a woman. Since that time the honor of leaving the church first was accorded to the female worshippers.

"About the time of the first World War this rite was discontinued," admitted J. J. Figi, treasurer of the Evangelical and Reformed Church. "But in a free country like this it has become of little significance."

All Swiss cannot be farmers, neither in the old country nor in the United States. It is for this reason that many have become proficient in woodcarving, embroidery and watchmaking. New Glarus has the only lace factory west of the Alleghenies. The delicate tracery of the varied patterns offers designs of exquisite beauty in laces, ruchings, curtains, embroidery, handkerchiefs and aprons made in native Swiss styles. Among the Milwaukee Swiss, who number 5,000, I found artists in woodcarving and one Swiss watchmaker who had learned his trade after several years of exacting study in a college for watchmakers in Neuchatel, Switzerland.[39]

The Swiss of Wisconsin are a sociable people. New Year's Eve is especially eventful among the families. Then the relatives get together for a visit. A serving of whipped cream, pear bread, and a little schnapps enlivens the dawning hours of another year.

Bridging the present and the past, there stands in the church yard at New Glarus a monument to the founders. I stood before it in the pensive blue of evening to read the family names — Aebly, Babler, Becker, Duerst, Hefty, Hoesly, Kundert, Legler, Schindler, Schmid, Streiff, Stauffacher, Trumpy, and Wild. It was a hushed moment that will remain forever as a memory of the Swiss country of Wisconsin.

Like a Stylite on his pedestal, a Swiss pioneer carved in grey marble overlooks the bustling commercialism on the village streets. With one hand shading his eyes, he seems to envision a still more remarkable future for a sturdy people.

---

[36] Luchsinger, John, **The Swiss Colony in New Glarus**, Wisconsin Historical Collections, Vol. VIII, plp. 411-445, Ibid, Vol. XII, pp. 334-382, Von Grueninger, John Paul, **The Swiss In the United States**, 1940, Madison, Wisconsin.

[37] Schmalz, Oskar Fr. (Editor), **Bi iis im Barnerland, Vierstimmige Volks-und Jodellieder**, Bern (Switzerland), 1929, is a popular song book found in taverns.

[38] For recipes of popular Swiss dishes served by Mrs. Esther Stauffacher, see Wisconsin Agriculturist and Farmer, July 13, 1940.

[39] Upright Swiss Embroidery Co., New Glarus, Wis. For story of Milwaukee Swiss, see Milwaukee Journal, January 30, 1941.

❖

CHAPTER VIII

Belgian Dust Dancers Celebrate
Brussels and Rosiere

A SOFT twilight was descending over the Door County peninsula. Along the highway, in the farm yards of the newly elected town officers, garish banners were waving auspiciously atop lofty Maypoles heralding tidings of a change in government. A group of women were trudging in pairs toward a wayside shrine, there to recite the rosary in honor of the Virgin Mary. For in the Belgian settlements May is the month propitiously dedicated to civic reorganization and spiritual rekindling.

A community lying along forty miles of the Green Bay shore, east to Casco and north to Sturgeon Bay, it is peopled almost entirely by Belgians. It is the largest rural settlement of the Belgian nationality in America. The compactness of the neighborhood helps to keep alive the language and retain the quaint customs of the old country. A kindred attachment in race and a loyal devotion to Catholic belief lend to this land the romantic spirit of French Canada.[40]

Every May Day the inhabitants march to the homes of their recently elected town officials bearing a balsam tree, peeled of bark, stripped of all but the topmost branches and decorated with colored ribbons, streamers, and an American flag. This emblem is anchored in the front yard of the home of the honored citizen. It is symbolic of authority and expresses a public pledge of obedience, not only to the laws of the state but to a custom which requires local and family disputes to be submitted to the magistrate for settlement. In turn the official reciprocates with a barrel of beer or the furnishing of a dance hall, that the well-wishers may make merry. And thus does custom of the land across the sea live in this singular Maypole "republic."

I drove through the settlements a few days after the celebrations. The town lines of Union, Gardner and Brussels in Door County, of Lincoln and Red River in Kewaunee County, and of Robinsonville and the Chapel in Brown County were discernible by the recurring appearance of official symbols in the dooryards. And in the hamlet of Brussels, nailed to the dance hall entrance, was a golden spindle that lost its plume in the gloaming.

Gradually my interest in Maypoles declined through a heightened curiosity over wayside shrines. These little prayer-houses, appearing often at crossroads, were as intriguing as the story of Chaucer's devout pilgrims told in the Canterbury Tales. I stopped to make inquiries.

"These are little chapels," explained Mary Baudhuin, who for sixty years has tended the little shrine of the Immaculate Conception, across from her farm home at the outskirts of Fairland. "People build these prayer-houses because of a promise to God if freed of some hardship or disease. Then, when illness breaks out in the community, farm women gather here to pray the Novena every evening. Always in May we come to say the Rosary."

"Are the shrines named, like the Catholic churches, after the Saints?"

"Just the same," was the answer. "If we were nearer to the churches we would not need our little shrines. But in our hours of worry and sorrow we have a place close at home to speak our heart and lay our burden."

The men of vision caused a Belgian community to be founded in Wisconsin that now has a population of over 30,000. A chance invitation caught the imagination of the leader. The office of immigration commissioner of Wisconsin had been created by the legislature of 1852. Gysbert Van Steenwyk, of La Crosse, was named to the post. The services of a German assistant were employed and a pamphlet in the Flemish language was prepared reciting glowingly the homestead opportunities offered.

One of these circulars fell into the hands of Francois Petinoit, owner of a small Belgian farm, who had entered a tavern in Antwerp.[41] Over and again he read the promise of the United States Government to sell land for only $1.25 an acre. He could scarcely wait to return to his home in the province of Bradant, in Central Belgium, to confer with his neighbors. Eventually nine other small farmers, like Petinoit, decided to join in the venture.

Disposing of their few belongings these adventurous colonists set sail from Antwerp on the "Quennebec," May 18, 1853. Aboard ship were nearly a hundred more from other parts of Belgium and Holland who carried copies of the same circular. For seven weeks their little sailing vessel was tossed and buffeted by hostile winds; during the last week the food was doled out and the drinking water was rationed. But the Belgian immigrants never lost hope. On shipboard they became acquainted with a group of sympathetic Hollanders destined for Sheboygan, Wisconsin. They decided to go along with them.

But on arrival in Wisconsin the Belgians discovered that the Hollanders already had the good lands selected for themselves in advance. Moreover, they had difficulties making themselves understood. The Dutch and French languages have few words in common. Learning there was a settlement of French at Green Bay, they re-embarked. There they found friends. Quickly they bargained for lands in the vicinity of the present Kaukauna, but before the deal was completed they met Father Edward Daems, the priest from Bay Settlement, a nearby French-speaking community. Himself a Flemish Belgian who spoke French fluently, he advised them to take up the rich, unoccupied area on the outskirts of his far-flung parish. Overjoyed with the prospect that they would be near the church of their faith and neighbors who understood their language,[42] they accepted the invitation. Lands were entered in the vicinity of present Robinsonville.[43] The community was known, however, as Aux Premier S. Belges.

Exultant were these pioneers over the outlook of becoming independent through their own labors. Letters were written to relatives back home. Soon they brought a fresh tide of immigrants. Then the hardships multiplied. Some of the new colonists had contracted ship cholera. The disease decimated the settlements. Food became scarce and the men had to hire out in the pineries to earn money to support their families. When at home they slashed the surrounding forest, converted the lumber into shingles, for which there was a ready sale, and cleared the lands for the sowing of crops. By 1857, because of unfavorable reports, the Belgian mass immigration ceased.

"We lived in our new home three years without seeing a horse," wrote Constant Delveaux, one of the first settlers of Brussels, before his death in 1923. "We finally saw one when Michael Schmidt went in company with his wife to start a little store at the bay shore. His wife was on horseback and he went ahead cutting the branches so she would be able to pass. We had big sturgeon and very good fish to eat. There was also good hunting and plenty of game."

The experience of the pioneer Belgians follows closely the Wisconsin pattern of settlement by other nationalities. There was scarcity, but no famine; there were difficulties in subduing the forests, but these were not insurmountable; there was homesickness, but the light of hope illumined their lives.

Faith brought them a guide. On August 15, 1858, among the Catholics of Aux Premier S. Belges there reportedly took place a miracle. Little Adele Brice was returning home from attending church eight miles away in the Bay Settlement when, between two small trees, a few feet apart, the Virgin Mary appeared to her.[44]

"Give me thy service in spreading the faith; build on this spot a chapel," she commanded in French, her hands outstretched in a golden light, as if bestowing a blessing. This direction occurred at the first apparition and was reported a week later on the same spot.

"How can I do that, my good mother? I am but a poor, ignorant creature myself," Adele answered humbly.

"Go and fear nothing. I will help you," Our Lady instructed Adele.

When the Belgian neighbors heard the story, they believed.

In answer to that command they immediately built a chapel on the spot. Gradually the place took the name "La Chapelle."

Churchmen arose to scoff the idea of an apparition as incredible, but credence persisted. Feeling herself divinely directed, Adele joined a nearby Belgian sisterhood. Soon the believers increased so much that an enlarged church had to be erected. Afterwards, a home for the care of crippled children was added. Now a modern edifice and school accommodate the diocesan demands. Aux Premier S. Belges has become a shrine.

Ancient church customs are observed. Annually on the last Monday in May, devout Belgians assemble here to petition the Virgin the blessings of abundant crops. The attendance usually exceeds 2,500. To the singing of litanies of special supplication, the Rogation procession leaves the shrine, headed by the cross-bearer in surplice and cassock, to wend its way through the fields. Little girls, dressed in white and wearing long veils, strew flowers on the highway.

Holding high the monstrance that all may see the Blessed Sacrament, the priest follows, wearing brilliant sacerdotal robes of dignity. As the procession advances, the choir sings beautiful hymns and the people fall in line. It is an hour of deep solemnity. Once the last straggler at the rear arrives at the chapel, the celebrants abandon festivities. Quickly they return to their homes. There is no feasting on this occasion.

Later on, each August 15, from 15,000 to 20,000 gather for Assumption Day and the anniversary of the apparition. The devout begin arriving at midnight to pay their respects to the Virgin. Each year groups of pious women from Green Bay make the seventeen-mile pilgrimage afoot in early morning that they may the more completely relive and experience the devotional ways of their medieval and pioneer forbears. The field mass celebrated on that occasion is a colorful ceremonial. The white vestments of the officiating priest and his assistants appear symbolically triumphant against the encircling green of the countryside. A choir of trained voices singing the beautiful Gregorian chants of the church touches the hearts of the listeners. As the services proceed, the people at the circumference of the crowd grow quiet and finally there comes a hush. I hear the voice of the priest begin the Lord's prayer in Latin:

"Pater noster, qui es in coelis,
sanctificetur nomen tuum."

Innocent, upturned faces of little children kneeling on the ground close by the altar bespeak in spirit the eternal words. The choir leader gives a signal.

"Sed libera nos a malo. Amen."
"Deliver us from evil. Amen."

Turning toward those about me I seemed to see their burdens disappear. They have come long distances to make this fervent petition.

Before noon a traditional procession, led by fifteen to twenty priests and bearing the Holy Sacrament enclosed in the golden monstrance, encircles the five-acre grounds. The route followed is that taken at the time of the "big fire," when Sister Adele was in charge and the buildings were providentially saved from the flames. Slowly marching four and five abreast, the people, reciting the rosary, wend their way along a lane bordered by the golden shocks of a harvest scintillating under the sun of high noon. People from everywhere in the region participate and pray. Trudging along may be seen the halt, the lame and the blind, and others bowed by sorrow, seeking a miraculous cure for their ailments — and some are not disappointed. Discarded crutches that clutter the chapel alcoves offer mute evidence. The Aux Premier S. Belges "Lourdes" has become a popular shrine in the Middle West.

Two visits twenty years apart have furnished me with lasting memories of the sights of the community and the fervor of the pilgrims. There has been little, if any, change in the interim. The chapel altar surmounted by a beautiful statue of the Virgin Mary is set over the spot where she appeared. For hours before and after the field services the devout creep around it on their knees reciting prayers. They are on hallowed ground. Only at night does the countryside resume its rural calm.

Not alone on these special days is the shrine visited.

Automobiles have made the chapel widely accessible. The Virgin Mary is a favorite patroness of the Belgian people. Daily, in groups and singly, come the pious and the curious.

"Petitions that formerly were made in our neighborhood prayer-houses are now taken directly to the Virgin at the shrine," said a crippled pilgrim in whom I took an interest on my last visit. He thought the time would come when the wayside shrines would be abandoned. I frankly told him I hoped his prediction would never come true. Since 1894 all parishes in the so-called Belgian Peninsula have been in the care of the White Fathers of St. Norbert, with headquarters at West De Pere.[45]

Upon no other Wisconsin community, however, did the tragic scourge of fire descend with such fury, devastation and death as it did upon the Belgians. Belgianland had attained a state of comfort when swept by the holocaust of October 8, 1871. The autumn had been unusually dry and the woods had become a tinder box; the harvest had been gathered in the barns and the corn was in the shock. A blue haze hung in the sky and then in a moment the air was turned into tongues of fire; the roar of the flaming forests was unearthly. The poor settlers, white as ghosts, rushed from their homes believing that the terrible day of judgment had arrived. Within a few short hours before the wind veered and rain fell a thousand people were dead and four thousand others were homeless in a fire-burnt district embracing four counties.[46] The beautiful country of the Belgians lay in ashes.

In their deep faith they accepted their burden as the will of God. In faith they rebuilt their homes; in faith they restored their churches; in faith they sought solace in their crossroad wayside prayer-houses. Faith is the outstanding characteristic of these people.

Beside the concrete highway midway between Brussels and Sturgeon Bay is a hill and valley section set aside as a memorial to the pioneers of that tragic hour. It bears the name of "Tornado Park." Before its entrance portals I paused with uncovered head, and in humility copied from the inscribed tablets this cryptic recital:

Here was the Village of
Williamsonville with a population
of 77 persons on October 8, 1871.
This Village was blotted out by a tornado of fire.
60 persons sought refuge in an open field surrounding
this spot and were
burned to death.

The sight that arose from the ashes was different. With pioneer log houses and frame buildings destroyed, the new homes, churches, schools, dance halls, stores and even barns were constructed of red brick. Tradition, inheritance and convenience prompted the innovation. Required to start anew, the inhabitants dug the red clay soil, moulded it into forms, dried it in the sun, and then kiln-burned it. New Belgium took on the foreign look of Old Belgium.

"Long years ago in Belgium we had brick houses," explained a pioneer farmer. "The people used them because they lasted longer and did not need to be painted every two years, like lumber. That is why we made the change when the time for rebuilding came after the fire."

Fascinating Old World ceremonials have been brought to Wisconsin by different nationalities. One of the most unique is the "Kermiss," held each autumn by the Belgians and others. It is a thanksgiving for a bounteous harvest. Beginning on the last Sunday in August these two-day celebrations become weekly events. For seven consecutive Sundays they follow in order at Lincoln, Brussels, Rosiere,Dykesville, Gardner, Duvall and Missiere.

Origin of the festival is lost in a remote past. The observance has been celebrated in Wisconsin since 1858. The very name "Kirk-Messe," or "church mass," however, discloses a religious connection.[47] Each event is opened after Sunday mass in the village church. Following tradition the first dance of the Kermiss must be held in the roadway — the dance of the dust — harking back to a recognition of the soil from which the harvests have sprung. The Rosiere celebration is usually accorded this distinctive recognition.

Only at Kermiss time is the old Dutch oven fired up. At this time there are pies to be made by the dozens and loaves of bread to be baked by the score. Slowly this manner of baking is being discontinued and modern methods utilized. That the Dutch oven will survive another decade is considered doubtful.

These celebrations set records for eating. Belgian pie alone satisfies hungry appetites. At the bottom is custard and then follow liberal layers of prunes and apples and a top coating of cottage cheese. At a recent celebration in a hamlet of thirty inhabitants, the visitors who came consumed 2,000 pies. One housewife baked eighty-two for the feast. I sat down and became a part of the scene.

Village tavern-keepers promote these anniversaries. There is dancing far into the early morning and drinking of beer until the last tired celebrant decides to depart.

Hospitality beams in the countryside. More than all else, these annual festivals promote a bond of true community spirit. Old acquaintances meet; new friends are made; the past is recounted. The Kermiss is the outstanding event of the year in the Belgian settlement. For it preparations are made with greater detail than for the coming of Christmas. Custom and tradition more often offer an undying truth which "moderns" erroneously seek to belittle as "old-time bunk." The gentling touch of olden days has a soothing influence on those who dwell in such harmony.

Unlike most Catholic communities the Belgians have never actively supported parochial schools. In the country from which the Belgians emigrated, schools, secular and parochial, were supported by state, province and town funds. When the Belgians came to this country they had not been trained, as had the Irish and Germans, individually to finance the education of their children. Eventually the Belgians learned that if they took part in voting they could have the public schools free. This policy they approved.

"There is no aversion to church-supervised education," explained Rev. J. J. Gloudemans, pastor of St. Francis Xavier Catholic Church in Brussels. "There is a reluctance in paying for it, when the public offers schools free. Wisconsin Belgians have never learned to support schools by their own contributions. But they do insist on instructing their children in the Catholic faith. We who have lived and worked here for years know that our Belgians are deeply and instinctively religious."

English is today the general language and all except the older people converse in it readily in their homes. Wisconsin Belgians who speak the language of the homeland converse in the Walloon dialect. The Walloon language is a French patois spoken in the provinces of Liege, Hainaut, Namur, Luxemburg and Brabant. The Hainaut, Namur and Brabant dialect is called "Namurois." The Belgians of Door County hail from Hainaut, Namur and Brabant, approximately in this proportion: Fifty percent from Namur, forty percent from Brabant, ten percent from Hainaut. Students of languages claim that the Walloon patois comes closer to the "old" French than many of the patois languages in France itself.

"Of those who speak the two languages used in New Belgium, more than ninety percent use the Walloon dialect," said Joseph L. Bouche, the cobbler at Brussels, who has held the office of clerk in the community for twenty years. "A few there are who speak Flemish. These we cannot understand at all. There is as much difference between Flemish and Walloon as between German and French. Belgium is composed of two distinct nationalities — the Flemings, who inhabit the northern provinces, and the Walloons, who live in the southern section. The Flemings are of Germanic origin and the Walloons of Latin."

Wisconsin Belgians are a thrifty people. Farming is their life. The frugality of centuries is born in them. While their homeland beyond the sea is only one-fifth the size of Wisconsin, their population is three times greater than ours. They are a friendly folk. Especially do they enthuse at ceremonials — weddings, christenings, and family anniversaries.

"The rooms ring with volleys of laughter when the Belgians congregate," observed Alfred J. Vandortie, a Brussels tavern-keeper. "They are very musical and carry their happiness in their hearts."

Bordering the Belgian settlement on the south, running

through Kewaunee and into Manitowoc County, and attached like a selvage of gold, is a settlement of Bohemians. My visits among these people reminded me of their kinsfolk, whom I found settled around Phillips in Price County. So similar were Bohemian customs to those of their Belgian neighbors that they have been assimilated — with at least two exceptions. Almost every Bohemian home has its own poppy garden to raise the seeds used in baking bread and rolls. Breakfast would not be breakfast to the Bohemians without the buchty and koblihy. On July mornings these little plots, aflame with gorgeous bright colors, make an attractive countryside sight. Moreover, while the Belgians charitably care for their aged in their own homes, Kewaunee County Bohemian farmers erect a separate house on the farmstead for use when the parents retire.

Only by accident did I discover this benevolent policy. Mistaking a country road out of Ellisville, I was wandering aimlessly about the rural district, impressed by the prosperity of a community where it appeared that there was a tenant house on every farm. At last, on the doorstep of the extra little house I saw an old man sitting in the shade smoking his pipe while the grandmother knitted. Similarly, at the next farm, a gray-haired woman was out in her yard inspecting the flowers.

This is not farm tenancy, I thought. It must be another Old World custom. My surmise proved correct.

"It is the rule among the Bohemian people, particularly in the towns of Montpelier and Franklin in Kewaunee County, to have two houses on every farm," I was told by Joseph M. Mlcviza, a member of the Wisconsin legislature. "When the father and mother grow old they make a deed, turning their property over to the eldest son, who agrees to support the parents and to pay to the brothers and sisters fixed amounts. As each minor becomes of age, payment is made of the sum set forth in the deed and the record is then satisfied. On the death of the last surviving parent, the Court enters an order finding the obligations discharged. Probably by the time the last payment is made the interim will have arrived for the process to be repeated."

Upon request, Mr. Mleviza brought me the deed to his farm. It was the common form used in the community. From it, I copied these unusual covenants that insured support and comfort to his surviving mother:

1. To give to mother one-fourth of all grains, potatoes and fruits, raised, grown and harvested on the premises.
2. To give to mother 250 pounds of fresh pork, each and every year during her natural life.
3. To provide a suitable coop on the premises for fifteen chickens, but not to feed the same.
4. To feed, pasture, and furnish stable room for one cow.
5. To have use of the small dwelling during the natural life of mother.
6. To furnish firewood ready for stove use, and deliver same at dwelling occupied.
7. To give free ingress and egress to well.
8. To give, in addition to the cash payments to be made to each brother and sister, one cow when each gets married.

When the Bohemian grandmother retires from the hard work of the farm, custom places upon her a higher traditional family duty. She becomes the nursemaid to the children of the kinfolk. She gathers them about her and disciplines them when parents are absent; instructs them in the tongue of their ancestors; recounts for them the folk stories and fairy tales of their forefathers; teaches them to sing the songs of foreign lands; enlightens them about their religion and inspires them with love and charity. It is the Bohemian grandmother who leads the neighborhood boys and girls to loftier goals in life. The moral yield is richer than that of any soil the children will ever till.

The sunset in the west flamed more roseate than ever as I departed from Belgianland. This countryside was even more completely foreign than I had envisioned it. Deep in my heart I concluded that if the charity of these humble people universally prevailed, the message of the Master would be heard by all men.

[40] This chapter has been read and corrected by Rev. J. J. Gloudemans. Ord. Praem., St. Francis Xavier Church, Brussels. He was ordained in St. Joseph's Church, West De Pere, March 19, 1900, and since Feb. 8, 1904 has lived among the Wisconsin Belgians.

[40] This circular in the Antwerp tavern was printed in the Flemish language. Those writing the history of the Belgian settlement seem to be quite confused in regard to language. Belgium has no language of its own — Flemish is Dutch or Hollandish and the Walloons speak a French patois which is more French than many of the patois in France itself. Also see Martin, Xavier, **The Belgians of Northeast Wisconsin**, Wisconsin Historical Collections, Vol. XIII, pp. 375-396; Holand, H. R., **Wisconsin's Belgian Community**, Sturgeon Bay, Wisconsin: and **History of Door County,**

[42] The book language which the Belgians had all learned in their old country schools was French.

[43] Robinsonville is an inland community ten miles from Bay Settlement and four miles south of Dyckesville, on County Trunk K. Because of the prominence of the church and shrine located there, the place is usually designated on the guide boards as "Chapel." Robinsonville was the first post office named for Charles D. Robinson, editor of the Green Bay Advocate and an early day political leader. About forty-five years ago the post office name was changed to "Champion."

[44] Wisconsin Historical Collections, Vol. XIII, ibid, p. 385: Milwaukee Journal, Aug. 3, 1922, **The Chapel, a Wisconsin Shrine of Mary**, Sisters of Saint Francis of Bay Settlement, R. 1, Green Bay, Wis., 1943; other data gathered by author on visits at Robinsonville, August 15, 1922, and Aug. 15, 1943.

[45] Formal title: The Premonstratension Order, St. Norbert's Abbey, West De Pere, Wisconsin. Sister Adele died in 1896 and is buried in the little cemetery near the church she helped to found.

[46] Tilton Frank **The Great Fires of Wisconsin**, Green Bay Historical Bulletin, Vol. VII Nos. 1 and 2, January-June, 1931; Peninsula Historical Review, Vol. V, pp. 41-55. This conflagration is commonly referred to as "The Peshtigo Fire."

❖

CHAPTER IX

St. Patrick's Sons Don the Green
Erin Prairie and Monches

"E RIN Prairie" they call it! The afternoon of my visit, it was the busiest prairie one could conceive. The farmers were harvesting and the women folk were hurrying with the baking, for the next day was Sunday. The rural township is off on a side road six miles west of New Richmond.

Everyone seemed so occupied that I decided to motor about and to return when people had more leisure. Gradually, St. Patrick's Church, which dominates the countryside, drew me like a magnet. As I approached, it impressed me in size as a slightly modified replica of the red brick cathedral at Bardstown, Kentucky, the center of the first Catholic diocese to be founded west of the Alleghenies. When I reached it, the foreign charm in the religious devotion of the Irish captivated me. In a country where nearly every man passing the church door reverently tips his hat, where women and children come with flowers to decorate the graves in the nearby cemetery, and then kneel and pray on the sward for what appeared as interminable periods of time, the persistence of Old World customs could not be disregarded.

"Every monument except one in this cemetery bears an Irish name," said the youthful caretaker, pausing a moment in the mowing, "and that one is a Norwegian convert who had married an Irish girl."

Out in the center of the cemetery a statuary group arrested my attention. I had long been acquainted with the customary crucifix set found so often where Catholics lie buried. That is a re-creation of the scene on Good Friday. The Erin Prairie design was different. Instead, it represented the glorious victory of

Easter Sunday's resurrection, when angel trumpeters will awaken the dead. The soft afternoon sunlight quickened this dream in art into effulgent distinctiveness. The general atmosphere of the place and the devotion of the visitors impressed me as gravely cheerful. In their warm remembrances, the departed lived again as when they walked this earth. None were really dead, none lost in oblivion. Fate had gratified my wish and brought me unexpectedly close to the Irish heart.

Headstones lettered with birthplaces from every county in Ireland bear names such as Donahue, Kennedy, Padden, Ross, Gherty, Garrity, Maloney, Wells, Stephens, Murta, Riley, Moore, Dean, Mead, Meath, Gill, La Velle, and many more. A roll call of the same names at mass any Sunday would show people answering. It is as if the identical pioneers were still around laughing, joking, and praying. I looked upon it all with a feeling of sadness. There was a sting in my heart that told me this was Ireland in essence; the spirit of love, devotion, and hope.

"Erin Prairie has changed mightily since I was a boy," explained the township assessor, who had paused at the church. "Then the overwhelming majority of the people were native-born Irish or first generation descent. So many of the younger people have gone to St. Paul and Minneapolis, the Irish ways are dying out.

"There hasn't been a real wake here for ten years. Instead, two or three friends are designated to sit with the dead through the nights before burial. At least a part of the old custom has been retained. And it is at least twenty-five years since an Irish keener has appeared at any of our funerals. Customs may disappear but still a man would be a poor judge who would mistake an Irishman from Erin Prairie for any other nationality."

Unlike most other nationalities, the Irish who settled in Wisconsin came not as members of a colonist group, but as individuals. These first comers tended to remain in cities and were discouraged from taking farms by the priests, who feared that they would get out of touch with the church. A common bond of interest in those compelled by circumstances to remain at home, there to make a common cause against an unwelcome

British rule, a desire prompted by their faith to be near the early Catholic churches, and a reluctance to enter into mixed marriages kept them mildly clannish. Otherwise they would now be as completely merged in the common population picture as the Scots and English.

Large numbers of the early newcomers had resided previously in New York or New England communities. Before joining the general drift westward they had gained the status of American citizens. Before 1850 two well-defined streams of Irish immigrants were flowing into Wisconsin — one through the Southwest; the second through the Milwaukee harbor. The first Irish sought work in the lead mines. Many descendants are still to be found living in Benton, Shullsburg, Darlington, Seymour and Willow Springs in Lafayette County. The potato famine of 1846 and the harsh rack-rent servitude of the absentee English landlords induced the largest migrations. By 1850 there were 21,000 natives of Ireland in Wisconsin, three-fourths of whom had arrived during territorial days.

As a rule the early immigrants to Southeastern Wisconsin arriving at Lake Michigan ports settled in the lakeland counties. Three rural townships in Brown County were almost wholly populated by them. Milwaukee became a focal point for disembarkation. By 1847 there were over 2,500 sons of Erin in the Cream City, the larger group living on the east side of the Milwaukee River. Of these, the greatest concentration was in the aptly styled "bloody third" ward, a political subdivision, since conquered by modern Italy.

With Milwaukee serving as a distribution center, the Irish spread northward into the inland farming sections of Washington, Ozaukee and Sheboygan counties. Starting as a one hundred percent Irish community, the adjoining towns of Erin in Washington County and Merton in Waukesha County were slowly encroached upon by German neighbors until now the settlement has lost its outstanding Celtic identity. At its heart remains the hamlet of Monches, near Holy Hill, which alone survives as a distinctive Irish stronghold. A like capitulation has taken place in the townships of Emmett and Shields, northwest of Watertown in Dodge County.[48]

The third influx, the settlements in Northwest Wisconsin, came after 1855. Until the turn of the century, the farming communities at Long Lake in Polk County, Erin Prairie in St. Croix County, and El Paso in Pierce County were as Irish in thought and conduct as Cork and Dublin in the Old World.

Irish communities still significant are: Bear Creek, Winfield and Dellona, Sauk County; Fond du Lac, Osceola, Eden and Byron, Fond du Lac County; Elba, Dodge County; Meeme, Manitowoc County; El Paso, Pierce County; Westport, Dane County; Evansville, Rock County; Centuria, Polk County; Eden Prairie, St. Croix County; Lebanon, Waupaca County; and Poygan, Winnebago County. With the exception of a settlement in the township of Medina, Dane County, the great majority of the Wisconsin Irish came from localities now within the Free State.

Like the Yankees, the Irish were too impatient to clear stony, wooded lands. But comparatively, until 1900, the Irish of Wisconsin were an agricultural people. When some of the more restless could not acquire rich productive soil at the start, they took up work in railroad construction gangs and helped to build the first lines in the state. The graders on these undertakings found winter work for their teams with logging contractors in the woods; the regular workers became lumberjacks.

After the railroads were built, the next generation of Irish operated them. They were the Casey Joneses of Wisconsin, tall, fine looking men usually with handlebar mustaches. They were faithful workers. From manual labor jobs large numbers of Irish drifted into the cities. Twenty-five years ago the urban trek set in. If it continues at the same ratio for another century, there will be few Irish remaining on Wisconsin farms. With the passing of the pioneers, customs have been dropped quite generally and the younger generations are rapidly losing their Irish identity. At the present time there are over 50,000 Irish or their descendants living in the state of whom more than 4,000 were born in "the ould sod."

Traditionally the Irish are Democrats in politics. Politics attracted them, like moths to a candlelight, from the first. Five native-born Irish took prominent part in the convention that drafted the Wisconsin Constitution of 1848. They were the largest nationalistic group, exceeding all the others in memberships combined. Early attachment to the Democratic party came from a feeling that the Jacksonians were more sympathetic to the hardships of the immigrant.

One of the most tragic incidents in the history of the state arose from a display of their lively interest in politics. During the Lincoln-Douglas presidential campaign of 1860, a group of young Irish boys, members of the Union Guard of the Third Ward in Milwaukee, chartered the "Lady Elgin," one of the finest boats on Lake Michigan, for a round trip tour to Chicago. They wanted to hear their political favorite, Senator Stephen A. Douglas, speak. They took their sweethearts along for a holiday outing of singing Irish songs and dancing. On the return trip at night their excursion boat was rammed in the dark by a lumber freighter. The "Lady Elgin" soon floundered and sank quickly off the shore at Winnetka, Illinois, with a loss of nearly half of the six hundred passengers. That tragedy cast a pall of such mourning over the state that the disaster was remembered for generations in both story and song. It is still recalled by an annual requiem mass at St. John's Cathedral, Milwaukee, on September 8. My mother, then a young girl, must have felt the deep pang of community bereavement. Twenty years after this event she would sing her children to sleep by the sad words of a refrain taken from a ballad current on many lips at the time. I can recall but one verse repeated by her in ever softer tones until all was quiet within the cradle:

> *Lost on the Lady Elgin,*
> *Sleeping to wake no more;*
> *Numbered in death three hundred*
> *Who failed to reach the shore.*

Somewhat reluctantly during the Civil War the Democrats finally fell in line back of President Lincoln. Edward Johnson, the "fighting druggist" at Watertown, became an Irish patriot. During a temporary absence from his store, members of the anti-war element, which had organized an opposition to the draft, supplanted the American flag on the staff above the store with a rebel banner. Upon discovery, with pistol in hand, he replaced the flag and defied anyone again to remove it. This exhibition of devotion helped to make the community more submissive. When draft riots broke out in the Irish wards of Milwaukee, it was the Schweitzer bishop, John Martin Henni, who put the Irish back into line. After the Civil War they again became enthusiastically Democratic, only to break ranks when James G. Blaine was a candidate for President in 1884. To this day the Democratic leadership in the state has a strong representation of men and women of Irish descent.

Later when the Progressive movement was launched in Wisconsin by the late Senator Robert M. La Follette, the Irish endorsed his attacks on the political bosses. Heredity usually prompted their loyal support of the underdog. Their immediate desertion of the Democratic party left it without a virile leadership. For forty years the party was out of power, sometimes even without legislative representation. Meantime, in municipal campaigns, the Irish developed strength and demonstrated their ability as efficient city employes.

No other foreign nationality, comparable in numbers, has had so many of its sons and daughters enter educational fields. It would be quite the exception to discover an Irish home with girls where one or more were not teachers. There are numerous instances where every child in a large family has taken up school work. John Callahan, who has spent his life in the teaching profession and served Wisconsin as State Superintendent of Schools for over twenty years, is the father of three daughters, all teachers. And it was the teaching profession that became a stepping stone for many an Irish lad to enter the profession of law.

Rural Irish seem to have advanced more rapidly than the Irish city dwellers. Historically, the two communities of Meeme and Monches have left their mark of progress in state annals. From the country school in the Irish settlement of Meeme, about fourteen miles southwest of Manitowoc, have come men who have influenced affairs of both state and nation. No public institution in Wisconsin boasts stronger alumni.[49] Meeme, as a community, centers around St. Isadore's Catholic Church. It spreads into the adjoining townships of Newton and Liberty. The road map now designates the crossroads at Osman, but the name Meeme, by which the first post office on the old stage line between Manitowoc and Sheboygan was known, clings to the countryside like a burr to sheep's wool. Here the public school is so inseparably associated with St. Isadore's Church that people speak of both as though they were one.[50]

When other school boards were haggling over increasing costs, Meeme was searching for the best equipped teacher regardless of expense. Out of that country school came Thomas J. Walsh, who as United States senator from Montana was considered by the late Senator La Follette as one of the closest reasoners that body has ever had; John Barnes, a Justice of the Wisconsin Supreme Court, who retired from that body in 1916 to become General Counsel for the Northwestern Mutual Life Insurance Company of Milwaukee; Judge Michael Kirwan of Manitowoc; John Nagel, who was widely known during his lifetime for his editorial writings; Dr. Daniel Connell of Beloit, and Dr. J. P. Connell, who practiced many years at Fond du Lac; two members of the Taugher family who became priests and three others who were physicians, and a score of men who have gone into business in many cities along the Michigan lake shore. The Meeme country school was a debating club in which the families of the locality took part, when the word "community center" was unknown. Many public questions were brought to the forum.

Whenever I visit Osman, I walk leisurely over the church grounds. Across my way lie the variegated shadows of trees patterned upon the ground, as if men had left the imprint of their genius here to perpetuate itself in a mystical manner. The spell of association with their names blots out the drabness of everyday affairs.

Every visitor to the Monches community that nestles so serenely under the witchery of the tri-steepled church raised by the Carmelite monks on Holy Hill must catch a touch of the same rural quiet. But the Irish have kept aloof from the Carmelites, preferring to maintain their own parish church and individuality. The country school of Monches, at the lower end of that Irish district, has sent eight physicians, seven lawyers, four dentists and two priests into the world outside. And Charles D. Stewart, the novelist, who lives close by, insists that the Irish have so impressed their Gaelic that their German neighbors speak with a brogue.[51] My observations confirm the belief, however, that the presence of the Irish brogue is greatly overstated.

While Wisconsin's professions have profited from each nationality of pioneers, the Irish contribution has been notable. Besides teachers, its membership is rather outstanding in the numbers furnished to the priesthood and the bar, while the English, Scotch and Germans have supplied many of the early doctors. I have made many visits to communities settled by the Irish and am grouping together here, as best I may, the varied impressions made upon me. The word "brilliant" is more often used to designate them than the members of any other race. The name of the late Chief Justice Edward G. Ryan leads the list. Others who come to mind include the late Rev. A. B. C. Dunne, Eau Claire; the late Rev. Thomas Fagan, the late Patrick Cudahy, and Col. John J. Hannan, Milwaukee; Justice John D. Wickhem and Leo T. Crowley, Madison; Edward J. Dempsey, Oshkosh; and Daniel H. Grady, Portage.

Gaelic populations have always been deeply absorbed in legendary fancies and mystical creations. The vein of light humor animating the native literature accounts in a large degree for the poetic sentiment immortalized in the Irish character. Jeremiah Curtin, born in the town of Greenfield, Milwaukee County, became one of America's greatest linguists. He spoke seventy languages. Gaelic had a special fascination for him and he spent much time among the people of Ireland gathering folklore stories which he published under the titles, "Tales of the Fairies" and "The Ghost World." Even those Wisconsin pioneer Irish who did not read could repeat with feeling many of the old ballads and sing the Irish songs. The accuracy of their memories as to the dates of local events would stultify the written record; their exhibition of mimicry would convulse any stage audience.

A growing public interest in the Irish literature prompted the Wisconsin legislature of 1937 to establish at the University of Wisconsin a chair of Gaelic and Irish literature. The state and the university have both been fortunate in having as the incumbent of the chair since its founding an outstanding Gaelic scholar, Dr. Myles Dillon, of the distinguished Dublin family which has played so important a part in the political and cultural advancement of the Irish cause.

Extreme sensitiveness is especially characteristic of most Irish. Centuries of dinning St. Paul's admonition, "your conversation should be in Heaven," has developed a reticence on their part to make any reference to matters of sex, except in the most delicate manner possible.[52] Male stock are referred to by Irish farmers as the "animal," "critter" or "gentleman." This touchiness has gone to the point where innocent "joshing," when persisted in by friends, has broken up many a love affair, and the same affection may account for the numerous bachelors and spinsters to be found among the Irish. The consequent decline of the birth rate has resulted in the gradual surrender by the Irish of the laboring oar in sports and important posts in big cities to other nationalities.

Irish wives are jolly and make kind mothers. They will buy freely from a salesman if convinced it will promote the intellectual advancement of their children. But their sunny temperament allows them to sit down complacently for a visit with a neighbor in a room that is topsy-turvy. The Irish are light-hearted.

"Sure, I'll jig for ye, if ye come around tonight when my friend, Red Jack O'Connor, is over with his fiddle," volunteered Timothy Crimmins of Madison. "When I was young, I would have been the champeen except for a little error. I still have my old hat and fiddle that I brought over from Ireland."

That night I felt an exultation as I listened to the poetic wildness of some of these Irish tunes. Scarcely is there an Irish community in the state that does not have a typical fiddler, who plays his music by ear and keeps time with the stomp of his heel. Tom Croal, who lives near Hill Point in Sauk County, is generally accorded the honor of being the last of the Irish bards living in Wisconsin. His father's uncles were warriors on the borders of Ulster, near Donegal. They fought, sang and died for the liberal ideals expressed on their lyres and their songs of freedom have been handed down through the generations. Recordings have been made of most of Tom Croal's Gaelic songs.

There is another characteristic that kept astonishing me — the patriotic fervor associated with the name of St. Patrick. Of Wisconsin's 983 Catholic churches, the Apostle of Ireland ranks third, with thirty-nine churches bearing his name. His popularity in this regard is exceeded only by the Virgin Mary and St. Joseph, the foster-father of Jesus. Annually the seventeenth of March is celebrated quite generally over the state and on that day at least the descendants of the Emerald Isle wear the shamrock.

"The church gives special recognition to St. Patrick," remarked an enthusiastic Erin Prairie co-patriot. "If his birthday falls on Friday, a special dispensation is usually granted so we can eat meat and celebrate properly."

The Irish are good story tellers (shanachies), and few other nationalities can approach them for quick repartee. This may account for the success achieved by Irish attorneys as jury advocates. Simple incidents in life and apposite figures of speech embellish conversations. But the deferential manner of statement accounts for much of the enthralling attention the Irish command.

When I visited the Elba settlement in Columbia County, I was told the story of the Irish farmer who was a strong supporter of "Al" Smith, the first Catholic to run on a major party ticket for President. The religious issue had reached a boiling point and some of his German neighbors, who were supporting the Republican ticket, were inclined to use it as a smoke screen to counteract the attacks that were being made on the sordid transactions of the Harding administration. One day, following the trading of horses, the Irish farmer and his German neighbor turned to a discussion of politics.

"Isn't it terrible how the Pope is trying to get control of this country by electing 'Al' Smith President?" argued the German.

"Well, I don't know about that," retorted the Irishman, without a ruffle of discomfort. "If the Pope had wanted this country very bad, he could have bought it pretty darn cheap during the Harding administration."

A candidate for sheriff in Portage County had been told by his supporters that a certain Irish farmer controlled all the votes in one section of the county. Seeking out the leader, he was promised support if the boys could have a picnic with beer. This was readily arranged. On election night the balloting was strongly against the candidate but he stubbornly held out hope on the territory controlled by the Irish boss. But that too, went overwhelmingly against him. A few days later he met the Irish politician on the street and started to upbraid him for the small support accorded.

"How do you account for your friends failing to vote for me?" demanded the defeated candidate. "I did as I agreed, but did you?"

"You ran mighty well, sir, for a man the people didn't want," responded the Irishman, who, turning away, left the rebuked office seeker with this subtle observation upon which to meditate.[53]

An imaginativeness in thought inclines the Irish to satirize people with characteristic names:

> "A nickname fitting better than the
> name their mother gave."

One fellow suspected of stealing fowls was facetiously called "Turkey Jim"; the engineer on a threshing rig who seldom washed for meals was "Blackie"; three Irishmen with the same surname were distinguished as "Big Mike," "Little Mike" and "Black Mike"; Jerry O'Leary, who lived on the stony ridge, became "Hog-back Jerry"; Peter Goggins, the saloon keeper, was called "Whiskey Goggins"; two Norwegians because of their distinctive occupations and physical characteristics were "Skunk Foot Ole" and "Big Foot Ole"; the diminutive man who officiously served mass when the altar boys were absent was "Priestine" Murphy; the paunchy bartender was "Bullfrog Joe"; the cross old codger laborer was "Sealion Burke," and every lad with red hair acquired "Red" as an added surname.

For the third generation, the customs brought to Wisconsin by the natives of Erin have dimmed yearly. The ways of their forbears — as in the fiddling and jigging at weddings; the ghostly stories told at wakes for the dead; the presence of the grandmother sitting in the chimney corner dressed in black and wearing a white cap heavy with ruchings about the face — are only haunting shadows in the minds of most descendants.

But the innate habits of thirty generations cannot be broken in a century. The sunniness and serenity of character developed despite their long oppression are too deeply ingrained to be suddenly uprooted. The lightness of heart, poetry of mind, seriousness of purpose, romantic touch of spirit and lovableness of nature have made a leaven of the Irish as a rich contribution to the melting pot of Wisconsin.

---

[48] Desmond, Humphrey J., **Irish Settlers in Milwaukee**, Wisconsin Magazine of History, Vol. XIII, p. 365- Runals, Irene Margaret, **Racial Elements in Wisconsin**, thesis, B. A. 1912, University of Wisconsin; Whelan, Rev. Lincoln F., **Then They—The Story of Monches, Wisconsin,** Wisconsin Magazine of History, September, 1940.

[49] Titus, William A., **Meeme—a Frontier Settlement that Developed Strong Men**, Wisconsin Magazine of History, Vol. IV, p, 281.

[50] The present St. Isadore's Church and the nearby school are recent structures replacing the older buildings rich with historic associations of great men.

[5I] Stewart, Charles D., **Fellow Creatures**, Boston, 1935, pp. 318-319 Whelan, ibid, p. 53.

[52] Johnson, Rev. Peter Leo, St. Francis Seminary. has long advanced this theory from studies and observation of the Irish race. See, **Galatians**, Chapter V: **Ephesians**, Chapter V, verse 3. Also see Lord, Rev. John, **The Irish May Be a Vanishing Race**, Catholic Herald-Citizen, Milwaukee, October 11, 1941.

[53] This is one of many Irish stories told by Daniel H. Grady, Portage attorney.

CHAPTER X

Songs From the Heath and Heather
Cambria and Wales

IT is doubtful whether the name of any church awakens such sentiments of devotion in the Welsh-speaking world of Wisconsin as does "Peniel." Elsewhere, edifices of the Presbyterian denominations are larger and more prosperous. "Peniel" offers in addition to her white severity a romantic story of blasted hopes, slow decline, dogged persistence and gallant survival. Community singing, that has made the coal miners of South Wales renowned in musical fields, insures the continued existence of the Welsh influence so long as there is a Welsh farmer about.

Standing out in the open countryside twelve miles south of Oshkosh, with neither hitching posts nor village stores to share its loneliness, is a steepleless church that was founded by the Welsh settlers shortly after their coming in 1847. Girt round by fields teeming with fruits and golden with harvest in the fall, it looks as stern of countenance as were the Calvinistic doctrines preached every Sunday within its precincts. Its very name signifies a spiritual struggle — an allusion to Jacob's wrestling with the angel at Peniel.[54]

Peniel church is a small voice of such wide acclaim that, on the fourth Sunday of every August, Welsh people from all sections of Wisconsin come to join in the singing of hymns and folk songs. It is a day divided into three sessions. Once more the bards of the heath and heather stir the gathering, as of old, to scenes of exultant ecstasies. Hymns are their language of praise. The Gymanfa Ganu, as this observance in Welsh churches is called, has been woven into the social fabric of the state.

Faintly I heard voices on the air as I approached the August meeting. A puffy breeze suddenly gathered the distant words into resounding sentences:

"Onward, Christian Soldiers Marching as to War."

Assembled in and without the country church were 400 men and women arranged in groups—sopranos, altos, contraltos and basses—all eagerly responding to the directions of the choirmaster who had been brought from some distant city for the event. As noon-day approached the people warmed to the occasion. Greater enthusiasm became manifest. Then, like the quick whipping about of a wind, an exultant participant turned the orderly singing into an encore, repeating one of the verses already sung except in the Welsh tongue. Words no longer soared from the lips but from the heart. The whole congregation burned with renewed spirit. The purity of natural voices scored new heights. Again and again other verses were repeated until it seemed the singers' voices would break in the wildness of enthusiasm. The organist and chorister must always be alert to renewed outbursts once this "hwyl" (spirit) appears. Pausing only for meals, served picnic style from huge baskets, the festival proceeded. Darkness fell at last to send the people home. It had been a day dedicated to old ideals and new hopes. For me it had been a profound spiritual experience.

Peniel alone conducts the event annually. A circuit composed of the Welsh churches of Racine, Waukesha, Wales and Milwaukee rotate to hold the hymn-fest in May.[55] Usually the union meetings are larger, the enthusiasm more sustained. But the method of rendition remains similar in most of the Gymanfa Ganu gatherings. They are all that remains of the Welsh Eistedfodd, a great Welsh national competitive festival of song, which for many years was conducted at Cambria, as elsewhere in the nation.

The Gymanfa Ganu is the voice of Old Wales in Wisconsin.

"We have determined that the beauty and poetic appeal of these old hymns shall not die," said Hugh R. Jones, of Madison, a well-informed Welsh American. "Congregational music is needed. It will be the contribution of my people to the Protestant churches of America."

The Welsh are more easily traced to their new homes in Wisconsin than the English and Scotch. Loyal to the British crown, they nevertheless were not members of the Anglican church. Alike to many other immigrant stocks the Bible was a compass. Objection to paying tithes for the support of the state religion was a moving reason for Welsh emigration. Probably nine-tenths of those who came between 1840 and 1850 were dissenters — Calvinistic Methodists, Baptists and Congregationalists. The economic pressure of the landlords crystallized their dissatisfaction.

Arriving in Wisconsin in groups, they settled in some of the best farming districts. Often the lay of the land influenced their selection. Accustomed to hill and valley outlooks in Wales, they chose a similarity of landscape in Wisconsin. The first settlement was made in Racine in 1840. As newcomers arrived, they spread into the "Kettle Moraine" country around Waukesha and Wales. From there they pushed into Ixonia and Watertown in Jefferson County; Barneveld, Rewey, and Dodgeville in Iowa County; Spring Green in Sauk County; Bangor in La Crosse County; Sparta in Monroe County, and Wild Rose in Waushara County.[56] There are probably 10,000 people of native or Welsh descent living in Wisconsin.

For many years much of the rich farming section between Columbus and Beaver Dam was owned by the Welsh. Proscarion, once a distinctive community northwest of Randolph, in the southern part of Green Lake County, would no more be missed by a visiting Welsh minister than St. David's Cathedral would be omitted on a tour of the homeland. The northeastern part of Columbia County was colonized by a ten-family immigration conducted from Racine in 1844. Cambria became the center of their religious and intellectual activities. To the west of the village a solid occupation of the farming lands resulted in the naming of "Welsh Prairie." There was founded the Zion Welsh church (1847-1930) a pioneer edifice of considerable renown. More recently the site has been appropriately marked.

The life of the Welsh has always revolved around their churches. They observe the Sabbath strictly, oppose dancing for the young except under school supervision, and are active in temperance work. Their ministers, Sunday schools and hymn singing have rescued the language and individuality of the Welsh from the ruthless fate of assimilation. Thoughts of this kind, gathered from history, were in my mind as I left Madison. Soon I was running along highways bordered by purple thickets of wild bergamot, sprinkled with black-eyed Susans, and was entering the hill and dale country of Columbia County. The peace and color of the landscape allured me. People who live amid magnificent surroundings do not always appreciate them.

Cambria, a village of 700, is still distinctively Welsh. Although Germans, English, Scotch and Irish have settled among them, a considerable percentage of the population clings to the ways of Wales. More than sixty percent can converse in the native tongue. Since the language has not been taught for a long time in either the home or the Sunday school, the survival of Welsh traditions and spirit is remarkable. But even if their language and folk lore were forgotten, their names would still betray their nationalistic origin.

When first I planned to visit there, I was directed to call on John Jones and family, out in the country. They were reputed to have long cherished the customs of the old and to have insisted to the last that the Eistedfodd be retained as an important national institution. Now, I was near to Cambria. But how to find the Jones family became a problem. There were thirty-three "Joneses" in the community. There were three with the surname "John."

"Did you ever hear him called John Jones-Tanyrallt?" inquired the cheesemaker, endeavoring to assist me. Upon my increasing bewilderment, he asked if I knew whether Mr. Jones lived on the brow of a hill. All the time the mystery was deepening for me.

"I think you must want to see John E. Jones-Tanyrallt," he added. "I will give you the directions to his farm."

"But, I want to visit John Jones, not John Jones-Tanyrallt," I protested.

"'Tanyrallt' is just a handle on the Jones name for distinction," he interposed, drawing a road map for me to follow.

I found the Jones farm home at the base of a hill in undulating countryside not unlike the valleys of Wales. Afterwards I learned that the first settler had located his home there for that very reason. The house was built in 1854. When told of my confusion over finding them, they had a good laugh. I had tripped and fallen face down upon one of the most distinctive family customs the Welsh have brought to Wisconsin.

"Almost every farm has a Welsh name," explained Mrs. Annamary Jones. "Because our farm is under the slope of the hill, it has always been called 'Tanyrallt,' which is the Welsh descriptive word for that location. And, so that our checks at the bank are properly charged, since there are so many Joneses, we use the farm name also in the signature. Not far from here are other farms with significant names: 'Coed Mawr' (the big woods); 'Tred Dolphin' (a village in Wales); 'Ty Bricks' (the brick house); 'Snowden' (the highest mountain in Wales); 'Vron Haelog' (sunnyslope) and 'Tanybwlch' (brow of a hill)."

Less than a score of family names are needed to enumerate all the Welsh in the community. With as much fascination as the working of a crossword puzzle, they were charted for me with these final results:

Jones	33	Hughes	6
Williams	20	Davies	2
Rowlands	7	Owens	7
Roberts	6	Morris	6
Edwards	4	Evans	2
Thomas	4		

"But to make doubly sure," Mrs. Jones added with nationalistic pride, "the Welsh often use the same name over and over. And so we have our William Williams, Thomas Thomas, Owen Owens, Evan Evans, and many more. The surnames of Evor, Llewelyn and Hugh are yet preferred over the Hollywood designations."

Up a steepish hill overlooking the village of Cambria, made

doubly picturesque across the valley by the shining waters of a mill pond, I found the two churches attended by the Welsh from the village and surrounding countryside. They sit at an intersection opposite each other—one more English than the other. With the advent of the automobile, Welsh rural churches declined. "Portage Prairie," in Scott Township, "Jerusalem" in Springvale, "Carmel" in Courtland, and "Zion" in Welsh Prairie ceased to exist. Then in 1920 the Welsh congregations of Wisconsin affiliated with the Presbyterians as an independent synod. This closed more rural churches. Now the largest number of the Welsh churchgoers belong to village congregations.

Most of the older Welsh families of the Cambria community seem to prefer "Capel Mawr." It is an old church, low and Celtic in design, built in 1857. The serenity of age dwells securely in its shadows. The door was open and I entered. From that pulpit many a "Pregethwr Hen Wlad" (Old Country minister) has preached the gospel with divine fervor.[57] The Welsh are natural orators. From those pews now vacant has come many an accord, "Amen Ia, Ia." Welsh piety is often lifted to an emotional pitch. From that invisible assemblage I seem to share in the tenseness and fervor as everyone sings the final hymn, "Ton-y-Botel." Music is poetry in the lives of these people. Only in Randolph, Milwaukee and Racine is the native language retained in preaching and that only occasionally. Soon it may be gone altogether.

The Welsh are taught religion. At regular intervals, young and old are catechized in their belief at the "Chwarthoral" (Sunday school meeting). The Welsh schools of Columbus, Randolph and Cambria meet in rotation in May and October for questioning on the "Rhodd Mam" (Mother's Gift). Afterwards the adults are examined on points of theology that would stump many a student of Calvin. With Bible on knee, each must be able to cite the dominical authority for his contentions.

"We tried the new way of explaining the tenets of belief but found the results unsatisfactory," said Mrs. E. A. Rowlands, a Sunday school teacher. "Now we have gone back to the old Welsh method of examining people on the reasons. The foundation is better laid. Both young and old find an interest in the recitations of each other."

Later, as I strolled along the main street of the village, I met several men in band uniform.

"What's all the celebration?" I asked.

"It's band night in the park," came the response. "Better stay over if you want to hear a few good old Welsh pieces."

That gathering understood musical language. One rendition received three encores. Finally, I inquired the reason for the enthusiastic greeting of the selection in which some of the people joined in song.

"That's our favorite," an old man said, and all the time he continued clapping. "It's the Welsh national song, 'Hen Wlad Fy Nhadan' (Land of My Fathers)."

> *"Wales, Wales, favorite land of Wales!*
> *While sea her wall, may nought befall*
> *To mar the old language of Wales."*

I stayed around another hour but there were no more prolonged outbursts until it came to "Star Spangled Banner" at the close. Even then the crowd seemed unwilling to leave. Only when the players packed up their instruments did the people slowly disperse, their musical appetites apparently unsatiated.

I have since made a listing of the names of Wisconsin Welsh Americans who have become prominent in civic and business life. Three Presidents of the United States have given them recognition. Evan A. Evans, of Baraboo, was appointed Federal Judge of the Circuit Court of Appeals, Chicago, by President Woodrow Wilson; William A. Jones, of Mineral Point, served as Commissioner of Indian Affairs during the administrations of Presidents McKinley and Theodore Roosevelt; Joseph E. Davies, the son of an eloquent preacheress and poetess of Watertown, was named Ambassador to Russia by President Franklin D. Roosevelt; Rev. Jenkin Lloyd Jones was head of the Abraham Lincoln Center, Chicago; his son, Richard Lloyd Jones, Associate Editor of Colliers's Weekly, was the moving force in accomplishing the preservation of the birthplace of Abraham

Lincoln near Hodgenville, Kentucky; Peter Houston, who came to the Welsh settlement of Cambria in the early '40s with his parents, became the inventor of the folding film roll of the Kodak, later purchased by George Eastman, out of which the latter made himself a multimillionaire; Frank Lloyd Wright, of "Taliesen," near Spring Green, is an architect with an international reputation in his profession; Silas Evans, son of an early Welsh minister of Cambria, was long the president of Ripon College; John D. Jones, Racine, former Commissioner of Agriculture in Wisconsin, is now associated with Hoard's Dairyman of Fort Atkinson, and is a regent of the University of Wisconsin.

Awakening the next morning, I was conscious of a desire to spend additional vacation days visiting the Welsh. The warmth of their hospitality was a call that grew louder and more insistent until I found myself on my way to Waukesha. There the Welsh Americans were already making plans for the celebration of St. David's Day, which would not occur until March 1 [58] following. This is an annual event observed with marked festivities.

"Saint David is the patron of Wales," observed a medical missionary of the Welsh Presbyterian church who had just returned from three years of service in Africa. "This man saved Wales from the beliefs of religious fanatics. The Saint's logic disproved the heresy that there was no original sin."

A supper with a noted speaker and Welsh music on the harp, their national instrument, are the usual ways of commemoration. Sometimes there is a reading of poetry, of which the Welsh are particularly fond. Randolph, Waukesha and Racine serve some of the Welsh dishes on this occasion — Bara brith (raisin bread), cold leg of mutton with mint sauce, beef, baked potatoes, jam, caws (cheese), cacan branw (brown cake), and tee (black tea) . Sometimes instead of cake there is a serving of individual mince pies, baked in muffin tins, and often the celebrants ask for buttermilk, which is a popular Welsh drink.

There were so many Welsh people to call on that the afternoon was wearing away when at one home the hostess surprised me with an afternoon lunch. On a beautiful china plate that bore the pink representation of "Mary and her lamb" was a serving of brechdan dena (thinly sliced bread already spread), bara ceirch (oatmeal bread), caws (cheese), currant jelly, and tee (black tea) in a dainty china cup.

"This is a little afternoon Welsh luncheon like we serve often at the gathering of 'Helping Hands' — an assemblage of women to promote missionary work," explained the hostess.

As I examined the delicious thin sandwiches of white and oatmeal bread, the hostess explained that the bara ceirch is probably the most typical of all Welsh baking. Equal parts of melted butter and water are mixed with the oatmeal. The dough is rolled to the thinness of paper and baked.

"Were you planning on attending the funeral at Wales this afternoon?" she inquired. "A man once prominent in the community is to be buried. You will hear some beautiful Welsh singing at the grave."

"If I may be excused I will go at once," I remarked.[59]

"There is plenty of time. On your way over you should drive down Welsh valley and view some of the old homes of the pioneers. A visitor from Wales last week told us that 'Ochr Foel,' the home of the late John L. Williams, is just like one by the same name he had often visited in Old Wales."

From a high hill the Williams farmstead, with its sprawling barns and little white cottage set on a knoll, satisfied my desire for a picture. All about were old homes of Welsh pioneers — some neglected, others in the hands of encroaching nationalities, and the remaining few distinctively Welsh — clean and well-kept but flowerless.

The funeral cortege had entered Salem cemetery when I arrived. Crowded about the grave were more than a hundred people. Before the committal, at the signal of a leader, "Babel," the appealing "Resurrection Hymn" was sung. All the neighbors joined. Song lifted from heavy hearts the burden of sorrow. Something in the majestic melody of the Welsh voices, the challenging tones of the bass singers in the chorus, gave to the scene a deep solemnity. It glorified a fulfillment of the prophecy that life is eternal. It was a rededication to faith.

"There will be many wonders,
On the Resurrection Day,
When saints in countless numbers
Shall come in grand array —
All in their white apparel
Without a taint of gloom,
Resembling their Redeemer
Ascending from the tomb."

Driving out of Wales early that evening, I saw the pastor and his wife entering the home of the bereaved family. Welsh custom suggests the propriety of their dining with near relatives of the deceased on the evening of the day of the burial.

The Welsh are a sunny people. Their lives are vocal. In joy and in sorrow they find solace in song. At the first suggestion, the Welsh will gather to tear off a Handel, an oratorio or an old madrigal. Often I have visited with a stocky Welshman living near Peniel church who looks more like a bard from the heath than a Wisconsin farmer.

"Sing me an old Welsh song before I leave," I suggested at our last interview.

Drawing a miniature tuning fork from his pocket, he struck it against a chair and finding the note, began —

"O! aros gyda ni,
Ein Ior a'n Ceidwad cu!
Os cawn dy wedd, nid ofnwn fraw —
O! aros gyda ni.[60]

England spent centuries attempting to assimilate Wales and failed. So far the Celtic races have been unconquerable. Although intermarriage with other nationalities in Wisconsin has weakened the Welsh faith, the music in their hearts remains unstilled.

The songs of the Welsh will outlive the story of their migration from lands across the sea. Even the hills where they dwell give back the echo of their happy voices.

[54] **Genesis,** Chapter XXXII, Verse 30. Most of the attendants of Peniel Church live in the Town of Nekimi, Winnebago County, P. O. Pickett, Wisconsin. The church is on County Trunk FF, west one-half mile off U. S. Highway 26. This road is the division line between Winnebago and Fond du Lac counties.

[55] **Favorite Hymns,** Gymanfa Ganu, Wisconsin.

[56] Phillips, Laura J., **The Colonization of Wisconsin by the Welsh,** 1910, thesis, Ph. B., University of Wisconsin, in State Historical Library. State census, 1905, shows 2,811 Welsh foreign-born and 10,603 Welsh children American-born. Welsh no longer are listed separately in the U. S. census.

[57] Old Country preachers "sing" their sermons. In a moderately high pitched tone, the preacher carries his sermon, on and on, just as the high Episcopalian priest chants his mass, only the Welsh preaching is thus accentuated over a longer service than the relatively short chant of the English or the Roman mass.

[58] Baring-Gould, Rev. S., **Lives of the Saints,** including English Martyrs, Cornish and Welsh Saints, London, Vol. III, pp. 10-15.

[59] Williams, Daniel Jenkins, **The Welsh Community of Waukesha County,** with an introduction by President Silas Evans of Ripon College (1926) Price, Sadie Rowlands **The Welsh of Waukesha County,** Wisconsin Magazine of History, Vol. XXVI, No. 3, pp. 323-332.

[60] Blest be the tie that binds
Our hearts in Christian love
The fellowship of kindred minds
Is like to that above.

CHAPTER XI

Iceland Fishermen Go Seafaring
Washington Island

Two brawny, roughly dressed fellows were unwinding nets from a creaking reel and arranging them in baskets in a dark, stuffy, weather-stained shack that smelled of dampness and fish. As each receptacle was filled, it was carried to a boat and stored ready to be unrolled and set for a draught of fish in the morning. Through a crack in the wall between the sun-shriveled boards, the men would peer occasionally at the waters of Lake Michigan, tossing but ceaselessly approaching for their eternal attack on the shoreline.

As I entered through the half-open door, they were chatting, fisherman-fashion, over the catch of the morning. For some time my presence went unnoticed.

"More than forty boxes went out from the island on the afternoon ferry," the older man was saying as he removed his pipe, holding it in one hand as he talked. With the other hand he mechanically continued to arrange at one side of the basket all the wooden floats strung along the top of the net. Meantime, with seeming unconcern, his youthful helper would spread the web full across the opening, folding it forward and back. Finally the reel was unwound, but before removing the basket to the boat the youth paused and made a sudden response to the elder's observation.

"Not so bad! Not so bad!" he tardily commented, and as he turned toward me I observed the strong muscles in his arms, the powerful frame of body, and the almost childlike expression on his face. The lad was a splendid specimen of the Washington Islanders who call their home "the pearl of Lake Michigan."

"I guess that's the biggest catch this spring," he continued, again addressing the captain. "The boys who went down to try their luck off Kenosha will soon be back when they hear of this."

Both men now instinctively faced me as if for an explanation of my intrusion.

"I was at Gill's Rock when the boat came in," I responded, not desiring to change the conversation. "There were shipments on board for Philadelphia, Boston, Cleveland, Chicago, Milwaukee, and many other places. Are these the usual markets?"

"We've not been able to supply the market for some time," announced the captain. "But it begins to look as if the fish are coming back."

The interview was interrupted by another helper who blotted out the afternoon sunlight at the door, as he trudged haltingly into the room bearing another reel of netting that had been drying outside. While he hoisted it on the frame for unreeling, I went outside to look about. There I counted six other reels upended in the sun for drying and noticed for the first time, leaning in a row along the side of the building, buoys bearing red flags used for marking the net locations when set in deep waters. Momentarily I paused to survey the awkward collection of tarnished buildings in the hollow of Gasoline Town.

"How far out from Washington Island must you go to fish?" I interrupted as they resumed their unwinding.

"Twenty miles out in Lake Michigan at least," responded the captain, laying his pipe aside. "If you want to go along, you'll have to get up early and be here before five o'clock."

Gasoline Town on Washington Harbor was already deserted by fishermen when I arrived early the next morning. On the fresh breeze, I heard the cough of their vanishing motors. As I approached closer to the wharf through lanes of low bushes, festooned with dew-gemmed spider lace, disturbed squirrels broke the sleepy silence of glorious dawning to protest from treetops my early intrusion. Although I strained my eyes across the blue sun-flecked surface, I gained neither sight nor shadow of the departing launches.

Turning to my companion, Ben Johnson, a Washington

Islander from Iceland since 1887, I stood a long time on the dock in silence looking across to Boyer's Bluff, watching the dark shade of the cedars and foliage on the precipitous limestone ledge brighten as the sun mounted.

"Gudmund Gudmunder gave this island its fishing start," he began slowly, and I knew the reminiscent mood was on. "His son Tom still operates from here. That's his boat 'Hans' over in the mooring. Another son is a partner of Haldon Johnson in the fishing boat 'Islander.' Their father fished out of this place every day for over forty years, and then retired to remain the patriarch of the island until his death in 1935."[61]

Gradually the story unraveled, like the nets on the reel the night before, of the coming of the Icelanders. The blood of the Vikings who conquered Iceland eleven centuries ago — the Sigurdsons, Gudmunders, Einarsons, Gunnlaugssons and Gudmundsens — also settled this faraway community. Gudmund Gudmunder repeated his own story to his friends before his death and it was written down at the time. From one of them I obtained this copy:

"An Icelandic gentleman and the Danish consul in Milwaukee had married sisters. And so it came that the Icelander went to visit his kinsmen in Milwaukee. He wrote back to Iceland and this is what he said:

> *'All the gold in the mountains of California cannot equal the wealth that is to be found in the waters of Lake Michigan.'*

"He meant fish.

"I was a young man living on the south coast of Iceland, where my family had moved from my childhood home in the shadows of Mount Hekla. I was thirty years old, a fisherman and a net-maker, and I had my own fishing boat. I heard the letter from Milwaukee read aloud, and I decided to see for myself if the fishing were as good as the letter said. So I came across the sea, although my friends in Iceland feared I would be scalped by Indians in the little known, to us, regions of Wisconsin. That was in 1869. For a year I fished at Jones Island, Milwaukee. The next summer I was one of a crew of four who took a fishing boat up to the Door of Death. We landed on Washington Island and found the fishing good. So I settled here."

Gudmunder's letters to friends back in Iceland stirred up interest. Fourteen others came across the seas at various times to join him:[62]

Sigurd Sigurdson	John Gunnlaugsson
Hannes Johnson	Peter Gunnlaugsson
Arni Gudmundsen	"Yes-Yes" Einarson
Jan Nichol	Tom Einarson
John Gislason	John Einarson
Hans Johnson	Magnus Johnson
John Johnson	Arni Gudmundsen Le Grove

Washington Island is an ink spot on the map six miles off the blunt penpoint of the Door County peninsula. It is a government township nearly six miles square, twenty-five miles from the shoreline of northern Michigan. Millions of years ago it was a part of the Wisconsin mainland, but some geological cataclysm split it off.

Porte des Mortz, the French called the intervening gap of water. After the loss of 300 tribesmen one dark stormy night in the long ago the Indians knew it as a death trap and shunned it, if possible, believing it to be infested with an evil spirit. Its maleficent reputation as Death's Door has not improved since white settlers arrived. It is a treacherous channel, one hundred fifty feet deep. On calm, bright days its waters are of captivating blue. In moments of storm they suddenly assume an angry mien, splashing, moaning and seething with destructive fury. La Salle's famous "Griffin," freighted with the bounty of the explorer's expedition, was lost near this strait in 1679. Scores of trappers, traders and adventurous inhabitants have been caught and drowned in its alluring grasp since civilization came. Near the shore of Plum Island, where a government lighthouse blinks nightly to signal the mariner's way across, may be seen the rotting hulks and naked ribs of boats that water, wind and storm have demolished.

The "door" was the boneyard of many sailing vessels but is not so hazardous for the present day power boat.

These are animated waters. Threatened dangers are a special manifestation to those who venture heedlessly upon them. The summer sun attunes the waves into a musical song of rejoicing. Sudden wind lashes them into the wildest exultation for the sheer happiness of living. The eternal mystery of Death's Door is the haunting call of its waters.

There is a touch of adventure in the naming of the island. With the westward spread of the War of 1812, it became apparent to the federal government that it would be necessary to fortify the inland holdings of the United States if they were to be retained against the subtle influence of the British inciting the Indians to hostilities. Accordingly, in July 1816, three vessels — the "Washington," the "Hunter" and the "Mink" — were chartered to convey the Third Regiment of U. S. Infantry under the command of Colonel John Miller from Mackinac to Green Bay. Becoming separated from the other vessels on the night of the second day out the "Washington" put into an island harbor to await the arrival of the companion boats. After staying there three days the "Washington" proceeded to Green Bay, but its name has been linked with the island and spacious harbor from that day.

Most of the traffic to Washington Island comes by ferryboat from Gill's Rock, a hog-back of rocky land at the Door County tip, inhabited by thousands of sea gulls and a few fishermen. As the boat recedes across the channel, it looks more like the lost wooden shoe of some giant dancing about on the restless waves. During the summer, a regular morning and afternoon schedule that connects busses with trains is maintained for the accommodation of tourists. In winter, when the snow lies four feet deep on the island and the channel is partly closed by ice, only the United States mails are certain to venture. Telephone to the mainland insures daily by parcel post the needed supplies.

Vikings direct from Iceland, Norway and Denmark came to Washington Island to fish. They remained to build farm homes, where agriculture and dairying are operated on a scale sufficient to maintain the inhabitants. But fishing continues as their principal vocation. Of the three nationalities all are about equally represented, with a total permanent population of 800 people. A large percentage are now related by either blood or marriage. Summer tourists run the population up to 3,000.

A fin of rock, near the center of the land that old residents called "little mountain," makes the island appear from the air as a sea monster swimming the expanse of Lake Michigan waters. Four land-locked harbors — Washington, Detroit, Jackson and West — are the mecca for fishermen. All are inland, connected by good roads. Washington is a big bite in the cliffs at the north where the descendants from Iceland operate their boats.

Most picturesque of the settlements around Washington Harbor is Gasoline Town. Its weather-beaten docks make it appear as a strayed bit of Akureyri from Old Iceland.[63] Daily its air is bejewelled by the wings of thousands of sea gulls, who follow the fishing boats in with their catch. The gulls are an important factor in the island's life. They are the self-appointed sanitation commission. As scavengers they keep the docks and harbors clean. For this service they are protected by law. Off the harbor entrance, as the fisherfolk approach the dock and prepare to dump the waste from dressing the catch overboard, the air partakes of a cloud, shutting out the sun. The ceaseless, strident, clamorous cry, the gliding, dipping, fluttering and turning of white wings, as the birds skirmish to gather their dinner from the waters, is a sight amusing and fascinating. Once their voracious appetites are satisfied the scene becomes more serene. By the time the boats are unloaded every post and vantage point is perched by gulls quietly enjoying a siesta.

After the fish have been packed in boxes of ice and delivered to Detroit Harbor, the principal shipping place for the world outside, the men tan, dry, repair and pack their nets for use the next day. Tanning and boiling are necessary processes. The tanning is to darken the nets to make them invisible to the fish in the depths of the lake. The boiling is done at frequent intervals to kill bacteria and to remove slime from the nets, thereby insuring longer life. Fires are started under huge pans that look like the galvanized trays used in the making of sorghum. Into these the nets are dumped to boil, first having been sprinkled with washing powder to dissolve the scum and dirt. Afterwards the nets are wrapped on reels and uprighted in the sun to dry.

Washington Island is one of the richest fishing grounds on the Great Lakes. Millions of dollars in catch have been taken from its waters and the supply is far from exhausted. Fishing is the principal source of income for most of those who make Washington Island their home.

"It's more than a fishing island," interposed Arni Richter, captain of the ferry line. "At least three descendants of Icelanders who were raised on the island are now high salaried captains of vessels on the Great Lakes and there are many more captains and mates on fishing schooners. Icelanders are born to the sea."

Long before I came, I had pictured this Washington Island to myself. Nevertheless in the reality it almost seemed smaller but more beautiful. An increasing number of people are attracted by its natural scenery. Camp Breakers is an exclusive summer place for boys near Jackson Harbor, set in a scene of trails fringed with gentians. It overlooks Rock Island, owned by C. H. Thordarson, who boasts the largest library of Icelandic literature in America. This he is planning to install in his new island home designed in the architecture of one of the Icelandic Althing buildings.[64] Camp Pearse on the west shore and Camp Shuh-Shuh-Gah on Detroit Harbor cater exclusively to young girls.

Driving along the roads, viewing the homes of fisherfolk, I recognized in the artistic gardens, asters, zinnias, petunias and other familiar flowers. The timber on Washington Island is of second growth; the stone fences bordering the woodlots of maples and birches blend into an unusual picture. Sunlight burnishes the distant waters. The surroundings are glorious. All nature seems gracious, smiling and beautiful.

The Icelandic language is the pure old Norse or Viking, and is so little changed that school children in Iceland today can read the writings of 1,000 years ago. Many of the Washington Islanders keep abreast of Old Country news by subscribing for the home paper, "Logberg."

Iceland is the only government that has existed in peace for a thousand years under the same form of democratic rule. Washington Islanders have inherited the same spirit. Successful experiments in cooperation, good schools, and records in dairying mark their progress. The islanders own their own airfield, telephone system and fire protection apparatus. If there is a fire, the telephone operator simultaneously rings all 200 phones ten bells and then announces the place. All turn out for duty. There is rural delivery of mail to all inhabitants daily within three hours after it is landed at Detroit Harbor in the morning. The Island subsidizes its own physician by guaranteeing a minimum salary of $2,500. On call a surgeon at Sturgeon Bay flies his own plane in for emergency operations.[65] There is no work for a lawyer to do and no barrister has been invited to hang up his shingle. Everybody knows everybody else; they are one big happy family. Like all Scandinavian colonizations the Washington Islanders are mostly Lutheran.

"The peace that we have is both hereditary and traditional," philosophized an old Viking when pressed for an explanation of the islanders' singularity. "Peace on earth is God's gift to men — especially for fishermen."

A bright sunlight bathed Death's Door as I departed from Washington Island. The air was still; there was no wave music except that stirred by the throbbing engines. Out in the world of silent waters the scene became topsy-turvy. Plum Island appeared floating upside down — the trick of mirages.

Although I had seen these lands and waters in all the glory of spring and summer on other visits, the luxuriance of infinite tints of blue and the marvelous panorama of transparent sky awakened thoughts for which no words can express the emotion nor human soul escape the touch of finding itself exalted.

[61] Haldor Gudmundsen, son of Arni Gudmundsen, one of the pioneer settlers, read and corrected this article for the author. His brother, Theo Gudmundsen, operates one of the large stores on the island.

[62] Milwaukee Journal, August 27, 1922; September 19, 1926; July 24, 1932; Davis, Susan Burdick, **Wisconsin Lore for Boys and Girls**, pp. 218-239; Holand, H.R., **Old Peninsula Days**, pp. 85-104; Barton, Albert O., Chapter XXIX, Vol. II, pp. 123-125, Wisconsin—Its History and Its People, edited by M. M. Quaife; **Alluring Wisconsin**, by the author of this volume, pp. 337-353. A slightly different version of the settlement is related in the Wisconsin Medical Journal, May 1939, pp. 404-408.

[63] Ancient Iceland: **New Pawn of War**, National Geographic Magazine, Vol. LXXX pp, 75-90, July, 1941. Map and pictures. U. S. Navy landed at Akureyri, in Iceland, preceding occupation of the island in 1941.

[64] Althing is the Parliament House in Iceland.

[65] Miller, Dr. William Snow, Dr. Thordur Gudmunsen **The Icelandic Doctor of Washington Island**, Wisconsin Medical Journal Vol. XXXVIII, May, 1939, pp. 404-408; **Flying Doctor**, Milwaukee Journal, Dec. 15, 1940.

❖

CHAPTER XII

Swedes Make Happy Yuletide
Grantsburg and Frederic

SANTA CLAUS is unknown to Swedish peoples. Instead they have their own mythical messengers of Christmas cheer. The "tomte gubar," or legendary gnomes, who otherwise during the year have been busy warding off evil and protecting the health of families, now gather in the homes to become especially gracious. Particularly at this holiday time they are believed to bring good tidings to all and unusual favors to farmers.

Long in advance of Christmas the Swedish settlement in Burnett County and the northern half of Polk County make joyous preparations. For two weeks before the festival all thoughts merge in expectations of the Yuletide. During these on-stealing days the pulse of sentiment beats as strongly as it ever did in the homes of their ancestors across the Atlantic during the holy season.

On St. Lucy's day, December 13, the baking is begun. For the Swedish, the yule period is a time for sweets and pastries. Baking and cooking preparations are virtually a rite in these homes for weeks in advance of the holidays. Much could be written of all the different kinds of knackebrod — spiced bread, buns, meats and sausages of all descriptions and the variety of Christmas cookies, prepared in anticipation of the happy season.[66] Gingerbreads, cut in the shape of a goat, known as julbock, are made by the dozens, the quantity dependent on the number of youngsters in the family. Sylta, a delicious head cheese, is cooked, seasoned, moulded, and packed away in a cool place for curing; lutefisk is put to soak and pounds of polksgrisar, a kind of red and white peppermint candy designed in little squares, is stored in receptacles beyond the reach of children.

Every corner of the house is scrubbed, the silverware is polished and the copper utensils, so dearly treasured by the Swedish housewife, are refurbished. As Christmas nears, the rooms are decorated with twigs of fir, festoons of colored ribbons, sprigs of mistletoe; and usually candles in three branches to commemorate the trinity are placed ready for lighting in every corner. An air of expectancy becomes universal.

Out of doors the farmyard is tidied up. On the morning before Christmas eve, a fir tree is erected before the door, strung with electric lights, if possible, and decorated with baubles, loops of popcorn, strings of cranberries and colored ornaments. Replicas of scenes from Bethlehem are sometimes represented. Sheaves of grain are hung in the trees because neither birds nor animals ought to be neglected during this merry period.

Recently there has come a rebirth of the old fashioned holiday life in Burnett and Polk counties. A nationality appeal to retain the beautiful Old World customs accounts in part for the awakening. By the time Christmas eve arrives, a real festival spirit prevails in the homes and through the countryside. For Yuletide attractiveness this Swedish district stands unchallenged. Within the two counties, a community rivalry prevails with awards being made by localities for the most appropriate farm Christmas displays.

On Christmas eve the members of the Swedish family remain at home. No community activities, outside the household, claim any of their attention. As soon as the chores are done, the feasting is begun. After everyone's appetite for food has been satiated with such dishes as reesen graun grot (boiled rice, to which some families add raisins and serve with sugar, cinnamon and milk or cream), yula-bru and generous quantities of coffee, the family repairs to the room where blazes the tree. There the Christmas gospel is read, beautiful old carols and anthems are sung, and then some member of the group acting as the Yule "tomte" (Santa Claus to them) distributes the presents. Each package has a rhyme, funny or otherwise, that must be read before the seal is broken. Through the house there are sounds of music, mirth and bustle.

That night the dishes used for the feast of Christmas eve remain unwashed. Only after breakfast the next morning is the regular household routine resumed.

On Christmas day all must rise early to attend church services. Julotta, a name given to the Christmas morning devotions, begins at 5 o'clock. There is a reading of the gospel, a sermon, many old-time hymns, and prayers.

The holiday period is observed with special emphasis on religious observances — more church services, more elaborate grace prayers at the table, visits by the preacher to stress the religious origin of Christmas.

For nearly two weeks the seasonal activities continue within the homes. On the thirteenth day the trees are taken down. The festival time is at an end.

In buoyant spirits the Swedes of Northwest Wisconsin pass their prolonged holiday season in a contented land of pleasure and peace. In their splendor, these forms of celebration are approached by no other nationality. Soon I came to believe that it was the intense devotion of centuries that has created this mythical atmosphere.

The Christmas hospitality of the Swedes is proverbial. From them came the beautiful custom of gathering around the fireplace at Christmastime to watch the embers turn into the faces of fairies. They gave us the Yule log in their feast of Juul, when a great fire was kindled in honor of Thor. The Goths and Saxons called the festival Jul, from which have come the words "yule and yuletide." The great Yule log must have been a warming spectacle in the olden days when huge fires were built in the baronial halls and mighty men carried in the Yule log that was to last during the feasting. Only the name "yule" remains to remind the world of this strange blending of pagan and Christmas rites celebrated in the long ago.

The settlement of Swedes in the St. Croix Valley was the last of several unsuccessful attempts to gain a permanent home in

Wisconsin. After the Swedish colonization of Delaware in 1638 no further settlements were started until 1841 when twelve families, including several members of the nobility, made a beginning on the shores of Pine Lake in Waukesha County. They called their community New Upsala.[67] Accustomed to luxury, the newcomers could not adapt themselves to pioneer conditions and the venture ended in failure. Another futile attempt to found a colony was made at Lake Koshkonong in 1843 by Swedish scholars. Among this group was Thure L. Kumlien, a graduate of Upsala University, who attracted attention as a scientist. He came to be recognized by Agassiz, the naturalist, as the world's authority on birds' nests. His botanical studies have greatly enriched the scientific lore of Wisconsin. A granddaughter, Angie Kumlien Main, of Fort Atkinson, has achieved more recent distinction in similar fields. The Koshkonong settlement was soon overshadowed by large Norwegian colonizations in the same locality. Then for a time the rebellion of the South, in the '60s, temporarily checked the promised tide of immigrants. Among the 600 Swedes who had already come, patriotism was flush. At least 100 joined the regiments of the North.

When again the ways seemed safe for travel, it was the farming classes from Sweden who sought admission. Those who came to the United States after the Civil War were more land conscious. William Forsell, of Ostersund, arrived in the St. Croix Valley in 1865, and after correspondence in Swedish American papers in Chicago induced newcomers employed in Peshtigo to move and to settle there. But the great impetus was stirred by well-financed propaganda conducted by the immigration departments of the states of Wisconsin and Minnesota and by the railroad companies that had recently extended their lines into the west.[68] Most of the Swedes came first to Minneapolis. Optimism filled their breasts. They had left their homeland because of high taxation and the ruthless seizure of their little farms under mortgage foreclosures. The prospect of cheap lands that they might develop with their own labors fired them with enthusiastic hopes. The Wisconsin St. Croix Valley colonization came largely from the County of Smebacken in the Province of Dalarne, Sweden. Experienced in farming, these families were able to overcome the hardships that had brought disaster to attempted Swedish settlements by the more educated ones.

"The success of these peoples is due largely to the fact that they built their houses and then remained at home to work their farms," observed Dr. C. O. Lindberg, Grantsburg, a native of Sweden who practices his profession among them.

As the lumbering operations advanced up the St. Croix Valley, the Swedes followed in the wake, buying lands cheaply. Much of the scattering of these peoples is traceable to the ubiquity of industry. Ogema, Prentice and Glen Flora were developed by their kinsmen in the cut-over areas of North Central Wisconsin.

Immigration continued well after the opening of the twentieth century. But the concentration remained along the St. Croix Valley. Estimates fix the population ratio of Swedes in Burnett and Polk counties at over 75 percent compared with 1.9 percent for the state as a whole and with 3.8 percent of the foreign stock. Nearly 10 percent of the 57,000 Swedes in the state live in Superior, their largest urban gathering center.

My interest in the Swedes began several years ago as the result of an exchange of correspondence with Selma Lagerlof. She was their foremost author and the most popular of all Scandinavian writers among American readers with the exception of Hans Christian Andersen. It was from her "Gosta Berling" that I obtained the first impress of the Swedish spirit.

With them the past and the present are closely united in time. Some of the Swedish pioneers in the Burnett-Polk settlement are still active. The Swedish language is generally spoken, Swedish songs are often sung at entertainment, and Christmas would not be Christmas if all could not join in the hymn, "Var Helsad Skona Morgunstund." They attend the Lutheran and Mission Covenant churches as did their forbears and many send their sons and daughters, if they feel inclined to pursue studies closely associated with Swedish thought and religious convictions, to such institutions as Gustavus Adolphus College at St. Peter, Minnesota, Bethany College in Lindsborg, Kansas, and North Park, Chicago. On the whole, they are slow to forsake the traditions of the land of their ancestors. Politically they are not as active as the Norwegians.

As I traveled along Highway 35 near Luck and Frederic during the morning hours, I saw patrons bringing their cream to the creamery in covered buckets suspended from neck yokes brought from the old country. Within the homes I saw rosemaling on trunks brought from Sweden with exquisite designs painted in Swedish blue.

To their New World home the nostalgic Swedish pioneers brought many foreign place names. The Burnett-Polk settlement has small communities with such designations as: West Sweden, Faln, Carlsborg, Freya and Ekdall. One of the lakes in the community is called "Trollhattan" (Spook Lake). The late Swedish merchant, Sven J. Benson, has been immortalized in Benson, Wisconsin, a Burnett County hamlet on the Northern Pacific Railroad. Some of the Swedish homes are named to denote scenes of Old World significance — Bethlehem, Sjo Stuga.

Wisconsin Swedish farmers are not large operators. Usually their farms are small but they take pride in having nicely landscaped homes. The county farm agent who works among them finds them quite receptive to changes in farming methods, although they are inclined to be somewhat conservative from the standpoint of completely mechanizing their work with modern machinery. They are frugal, especially those who were born in Sweden. They follow a well balanced grubstake program in providing home produced foods; many smoke their own butchered meats, and the housewife does much of her own canning, preserving and pickling.

No sooner does the Swedish Christmas season close than the ski entertainment starts. These are community affairs. Within a radius of twenty-five miles are four ski towers — at Grantsburg, Siren, West Sweden and Freya. Hundreds become members of these local clubs and thousands of visitors attend the tournaments, which provide four or five competitive jumps at each slide during the winter season. Through these combats with cold and snow, nature has developed men of striking physical appearance — has stamped them with a stern physiognomy.

There must be much in these new founded homes of the

Swedes in Wisconsin to remind them of the country of their forefathers. Through their choice of lands one catches a reminiscent glimpse of the lake and bay country of Sweden. So many waters dimple the land in spring that one part of the settlement has been named "the fish bowl of Wisconsin."

On the afternoon of June 24, the mothers go out in the woods and gather armfuls of fresh leaves and shaggy bows, to be used as decorations and to scent the house with the pungent perfume of growing things.

"I cannot give you the origin of this observance," I was told by a Swedish housewife near Frederic. "It is so very old, I am not sure how it began. In Sweden the sun was still on the horizon at midnight and this was the longest day in the year. All I know is that we have always observed this day, probably in recognition of the beginning of summer and the budding of the forests. By gathering green leaves we bring the freshness of spring into our homes. It is still the custom at the evening meal on that day to have risgryn grot — a rice pudding prepared with milk."

The tender-minded find here much to awaken their romantic imagination. As summer approaches, the legendary lore of the forests seems to stir their restless spirits. As evening closes the end of an all-golden day and folds its mantle of darkness over widely separated forest areas, the plaintive call of the whippoorwill announces the curfew. I have never known a locality to be held by its people in more affectionate regard than this Wisconsin Swedish settlement.

Something in the wildness of nature enthralls the Swedes. The men like to hunt. If they find little or no game, the ramble is a success anyway; being out-of-doors has its compensations.

Swedes have a touch for the artistic even when it comes to hunting. Near Antigo lives Alvin Linden, a Swedish woodworker, who came from a long line of cabinetmakers and boatbuilders in Sweden, to make his home in Northern Wisconsin. There he has been able to fashion the gun stocks of his dreams. He went to the backwoods, but the work of his hands soon betrayed him. Gun lovers beat a pathway to his door. His craftsmanship is now as familiar to discriminating gun owners as a Stradivarius is to the trained violinist. There is a certain refinement in the guns he makes for them. The polished grain of the wood and the appropriate fittings attest pride of workmanship, which in the hands of the hunter quickly partakes of the marks of the owner's personal attachment.

"The unsuccessful hunter, tired of tramping when possessed of such a firearm, may sit down on a stump in the woods and admire his gun, and consider the day well spent, nevertheless," remarked the owner of one such treasure. An instinctive high quality of woodcarving is to be found also in useful articles made during the winter months around many a Swedish fireside.

The home plays a prominent part in Swedish life. There is a friendliness in the household, a cleanness and orderliness that makes visiting a real joy. The birthdays of neighbors are celebrated by the unannounced arrival of friends from the whole vicinity. These celebrations are much more elaborate than is customary with some other nationalities. With the cool days of October until early December come a series of church dinners for which the entire population turns out. Meat balls (koubullar) and lutefisk are on the regular service. Swedes have afternoon coffee parties known as "coffee klatschens." Fellowship and good will are evident in all their plans and doings.

"But you will come in and have coffee with us?" suggested a woman at whose home I had stopped to inquire the way to Falum. "The cakes are on the table."

When I told Dr. C. O. Lindberg of this unexpected hospitality shown to a stranger, he explained that the Swedes drink more coffee than do the Brazilians who grow the bean. "And there is no apparent ill-effect from the frequent use of the beverage."

"The coffee pot is always on the stove," he continued, "and friend or stranger is expected to pause even if it be to drink but one cup."

"A bread that reminded me of Zwieback was served with the coffee," I added.

"That's called rusk. All Swedes eat it. It was formerly made in the homes. Now a bakery at Rush City, Minnesota, bakes it and three deliveries weekly are necessary to keep the stores supplied."

While we talked, I picked from the desk a Grantsburg telephone book. Running my finger down the pages I counted, Anderson, thirty-one; Erickson, seventeen; Johnson, thirty-two; Olson, twenty-four; Peterson, nineteen; Hanson, twelve; and Larson, eighteen. These are characteristic family names among the Swedes — names that carry traditions. Turned into such shibboleths as "Ole Olson" and "Yon Yonson" when shouted by a wild football crowd, they become epithets that stir the blood of the Swedish players. On one rural route out of Grantsburg there are so many Andrew Andersons that the postal authorities had to list them numerically to keep their mail straight.

Afterward the doctor took me into his back yard to show me a rock garden in the construction of which he had spent years. It is a microcosm of the Javla community in Sweden where he was born and confirmed and where he grew to manhood. The Swedish countryside for five miles around has been landscaped to exact scale — the birthplace, church, blacksmith shop, railroad tunnel, and all unusual features in the terrain.

"When I grow tired I come out here," observed the doctor, as we turned away. "It makes me feel young to vision familiar scenes where many of my people and friends still dwell."

The Swedes have made of their Wisconsin homes a paradise where the good things of life beyond the seas are still cherished.

---

66 Much of the information here presented was obtained in interviews with Dr. C. O. Lindberg, Grantsburg, Laura Chells, Frederic, and the late Assemblyman, Erik H. Johnson, Trade Lake, Wisconsin.

67 Hanson, Mabel V., **Swedish Settlement on Pine Lake**, Wisconsin Magazine of History, Vol. VIII, pp. 38-51; Raney, William F., **Wisconsin, A Story of Progress**, p. 142.

68 Barton, Albert O., article on the Swedish Settlements in "Wisconsin, Its History and Its People," edited by M. M. Quaife, Vol. II, pp. 117-120: Benson, Adolph B., and Hedin, Naboth, **Swedes in America**, 1638-1939, pp. 92-125 .

❖

CHAPTER XIII

Children of the Midnight Sun
Maple and Superior

$\mathbf{F}$AMED for the bewitching charm that caught the vacation fancy of the late President Calvin Coolidge, the Brule River traverses the Finn country of Northern Wisconsin. The Lake Superior lowland, where these immigrants have carved out of the dark wilderness their comfortable farm homes, bears a striking resemblance geographically to Finland. They still call their native country Suomi, or Marshland.

It was a cloudless day of blue.

Leaving the main highway on less frequented town roads that lead to the hinterland of the Finnish colonization, I passed farms where fences had been built of blasted pine stumps that had been seasoning in the earth since the removal of the virgin timber during the period from 1870 to 1880.[60]

"The only language the stump can understand is the Finnish," the co-op storekeeper at Maple told me.

Acre after acre of wild land in this section has been cleared annually for cropping on hundreds of forty-acre tracts, until today the Finnish homestead has become a challenging hope for a more complete settlement of the fertile denuded areas of Northern Wisconsin. Among these dwellers farm tenancy is almost negligible.

These amazing people have wrought a noble pattern in pioneering. The first Finns to come were migratory workers who followed the vast logging and building industries. Their interests were economic. Sufficient numbers had congregated in Superior by 1889 to found the Apostolic Lutheran Church. Soon Finns of different beliefs established two other Lutheran branches — the Finnish synod and the Evangelical.

The earliest settler to the Oulu district, four miles north of Iron River, now reputed to be the most densely populated rural township in Wisconsin, arrived in 1889. Depression in the iron mines of Michigan drove many of the Finns into farming.[70] From then on the numbers arriving in Northern Wisconsin increased annually until 1905, when the peak of the influx was reached. Many of these later immigrants, however, came directly from Finland for a different reason than the pioneers. They were restless young men who had become dissatisfied with both church and government in the old country. Settling here, they advocated decidedly socialistic doctrines along the lines of the Social Democratic party which was then in power in Finland. Some of the more radical of their numbers became anti-religious and eventually caused a split among the Social Democrats with one of the most vociferous branches (Industrial Workers of the World) forming a temporarily powerful group. Some of their activities were anti-social and caused the Finns as a whole to be stamped as political and social dissenters. This radicalism is still expressive in local affairs but in what is only a minor voice in the communities where they live. That section of Wisconsin lying to the north between Iron River and Superior and sloping to Lake Superior is most densely populated by Finns. The immensity of azure waters and the encircling distances of green forests seem to have conjured the strange silence of Old Finland to remain with her migrant children. On summer mornings the sun turns this far northland into a scene of reverberating blueness. The pines smell and the night dews on the underbrush exude a cool odor of freshness. Wild flowers weave a tapestry in the lowlands. The pioneer glory of Wisconsin lingers in this country solitariness.

Here nature, raw in its pristine ruggedness, needed a strong people, like the Finns, to make it submissive. Of the 15,000 of this nationality in the state, more than 4,000 live within this area. Iron County is second with 2,500, followed by Bayfield, Ashland, Clark, Price, Vilas, Barron and Florence counties. A considerable number of Finns are employed in factories of Milwaukee, Racine and Kenosha.

History deals with important events. Here there have been no stirring episodes. But all the time since the coming of the Finns life has gone on in its varied and intimate family details. Sauntering along the country roads, I became conscious of how little the story of these people is known generally, and I resolved to prolong my visit that I might appreciate these people more understandingly. My notes became more copious. I recorded some of the names appearing on mail boxes: Koski, Niemi, Maki, Jarvi, Ulvila, Ahola, Rauta. A more extended stay brought numerous surprises.

The Finnish immigrant is an ideal pioneer. He will live on the barest of necessities to get ahead. Land ownership is his hope. He is frugal, hard working, persevering, tenacious, courageous. Only a few may be said to lack pride in their nationality. Among themselves the Finns are neighborly; among strangers they are often reticent and cold. They congregate in communities because of their difficulties in learning English.[71] This clannishness makes their co-operative business enterprises successful. They have a passion for open, silent places.

"If the log house can be called 'architecture,' then the Finns have architecture," explained a Finnish banker in Superior. He was Ilmar Kauppinen. "The Finns," he told me, "have brought here a style of building which they had learned in their homeland. This has been more the result of necessity and utility than anything else. They found in the logs in Northern Wisconsin something they knew and understood, and they knew how to use the ax."

The Finnish log house presents an unusual piece of workmanship. It is a solid structure of hewn timbers carefully fitted together and dovetailed at the corners with finest accuracy. Partitions are mortised. Within recent years some of these structures have been changed in outward appearance by a lean-to; others have been either sided, whitewashed or painted. It is to be regretted that the native art is gradually losing ground because of the ease by which sawed lumber can be utilized in building. Many of the newer homes are more modern.

The resourcefulness of the Finns in solving pioneer problems has seemed little less than a marvel to me. Twelve miles east of Superior in the Amnicon River Valley is an old flour mill, built about 1900 by Jacob Davidson, a millwright from Finland. Its millstones were chiseled by him from native rock; he carved its big wooden gears by hand. Huge sails rotated by the wind were built to furnish the power.

"While they look much alike, there is a marked difference between a Dutch and a Finnish windmill," explained Mrs. William Davidson. "Dutch mills employed in pumping water have only four wings, while the Finnish mills utilized to grind feed have eight wings covered with sailcloth. Since the development of the country the operation of our mill has been discontinued. But for tourists it has became as much an object of interest as the nearby beautiful falls."

Finnish husbands insist on the women folk helping in the out-of-door labor. Specifically, they brought with them to this country the Old World customs that the women had to tend, feed and milk the cows. Cooperatively, the men get down the hay or straw for feeding and bedding the stock. Division of work still exists, although the younger generation seems less determined on the wife and daughters assuming solely the care of the dairy. Within the household in rural districts, however, the women weave carpets and rugs. The pioneer mother, be she Finn or of other nationality, remains a magnificent representative of the bravest spirit in the grinding metamorphosis from wilderness to a more settled civilization.

Other distinguished home features are more apparent. The Finnish farmstead is generally made up of as many as a dozen buildings huddled together. Usually there is a summer kitchen flanked with a good supply of firewood. In winter it is used for the storage of meats. Log construction was employed in the earlier type barns, but modern hip-roof structures are now becoming common as dairying expands.

Occasionally one will see scattered through the fields crude log buildings tipped slightly at the bottom, like a corn crib. These are the remnants of a custom of gathering and curing hay without hauling all of it to the farm barn. It saves much handling. Feeding is started in the most distant field in the early fall, but by winter as these outlying stores are exhausted the central supply becomes available. Gradually the system is being abandoned. More often, now, hay is stacked on an elevated foundation to prevent spoilage.[72] It is a method not used commonly by other nationalistic groups.

Of equal importance to the home is a specially built bath house (sauna). This is an institution with the Finn. A small building about ten by sixteen feet is constructed in two compartments — bath and dressing room. In the corner of the rear room a pile of stones shaped and laid up in the form of an old schoolhouse box stove, with an open place where fire may be started, is built up as a part of the dwelling. When these stones are hot, after about two hours of heating, the bath is ready. Then the members of the family enter in turn. Bathers sit on benches halfway between the floor and the ceiling. Steam is obtained by throwing cold water on the stones continually until the temperature reaches about 150 degrees. When they have perspired sufficiently, they scrub themselves with brush and soap, and then rinse themselves in cool, sometimes cold, water.

"Do you ever catch cold in winter after a steam bath?" I inquired of the storekeeper at Maple as he was about to enter the sauna at the close of his day's work.

"Never," he answered, "Many Finns erect their bath houses on a lake or stream bank, so they may take a plunge afterwards."

"A plunge afterwards," I repeated, with a cold chill.

But this was not all, for my informant added:

"Even in winter a douse in good cold water after the bath makes one feel like a king. To the frequent use of the steam bath I attribute the vigor and healthfulness of our people."

The bath is heated every Saturday and often during other days of the week. At threshing time the sauna is a daily rite. Newly constructed houses have a built-in sauna. So much a part of the Finnish home is the steam bath that bath houses in farm districts are frequently surrounded in summer by beds of flowers. The shower or tub baths are almost unknown among the older Finns.

"I can scarcely wait for Christmas to come when I can go home and have a real invigorating bath," is the hope commonly expressed by Finnish servant girls employed in American homes.

Beliefs akin to those held by worshippers participating in religious rites make the bath almost sacred. Older Finns prophesy that the person who keeps his silence while in the sauna on Shrove Tuesday will escape the summer torments of mosquitoes; boys are taught that the bend of the switches when lashed upon their bodies at the conclusion of the bath point unerringly in the direction from which their sweethearts will arrive. Cleansing is the outward manifestation among other benefits hoped.

Old World Finland offers an example of the institution of democracy. And in the New World the Finns' love for freedom, their common language and their unity of settlement lead quite naturally to their organization into labor unions, farmers' clubs, and consumer and producer cooperatives. In 1907 the first cooperative stores were organized among the Finns of Northern Wisconsin. By 1917 the idea had spread so rapidly that the Central Cooperative was established in Superior to supply the regional stores. This large concern, distributing a large percentage of its goods under its own label, is owned by some 125 local cooperatives, mostly grocery stores scattered over the northern ends of Wisconsin, Minnesota and Michigan. Groceries and household supplies have always been the backbone of the business. But farm supplies, feeds, automotive products and clothing are increasingly important. The managers claim that the Central Cooperative comes nearest to supplying all the necessities of life of any cooperative wholesale in the United States. Annual sales were nearly five million dollars in 1941.[73] Like the Swedes, the Finns also have their health cooperatives, credit cooperatives, burial societies, and even recreational cooperatives. Recently the Rural Electrification Administration was established among the Finns for distributing electricity. Through all history of the cooperative movement in Northern Wisconsin, the Finns have been the guiding force. But this is only a part of the story.

There is something intriguing about the personal interest the Finns take in their local cooperatives. They seek activity where they can work together. I talked with customers in the stores at

Iron River, Oulu, Brule and Maple. They answered my questions, with definiteness, as if they were the owners. A continuous advertising campaign seeks to inspire members to feel proud of their undertaking. I copied one sign:

> *This Is The Only Store In Town Owned*
> *By The Farmers. Your Co-op Is What*
> *You and Your Fellow Members Make It.*
> *Do Your Part.*

"What percentage of return do co-op members receive in dividends?" was asked of a farmer. He paused scarcely a moment for computations.

"My dividend on last year's purchases was about four percent. Besides, I think the articles purchased were at price levels lower than in competition stores."

"If cooperatives are so favored by your people, why is the liquor business left out?" I persisted.

"Probably for two reasons," he responded readily. "First, because a large element among the Finns believe strongly in the temperance ideal, and, secondly, because the law does not permit cooperative taverns."

Scattered through the Finnish districts are numerous halls built for meetings and recreation. In these gathering places a score of home talent, native language plays are given every year in the colorful costumes of the homeland. Often this entertainment is of a propaganda character, promotive of something favored by the sponsoring group. Many are the choruses and bands, orchestras and singing groups which assemble for community betterment. The Finns have their own cooperative park north of Iron River, where summer events are held. A similar park is located at Lake Soma, used by Price County Finns. While the whole effect has stimulated the cultural development of the Finns, it also has cemented their solidarity. They gather together instead of with other nationalities.

The influence of the church is not as dominant as in other nationalistic groups. Less than fifty percent (some estimate as low as twenty-five) acknowledge affiliation with some branch of the Lutheran faith. The influence of the Finnish press, however, is potent. Three foreign language dailies and five weeklies published at the "head of the lakes" keep these people in touch with each other and with Finland. Their difficulties with language are solved through the use of the printed word of their own native tongue. [74]

"The older Finn is frugal," said Mr. Kauppinen, whom I found was treasurer of the Workers' Mutual Savings Bank of Superior, of which many Finns are customers. "He has learned to take care of his affairs ever since he was a boy in Finland. He perhaps started working on his father's farm when he could walk, taking up more difficult tasks after he had grown up. He never had an abundance of money. Thus, he knew how hard it was to get it, and consequently he would not part with it easily. The older Finns especially dislike to buy on credit. Years ago, when the automobile became more and more generally accepted, the Finn would not think of buying one until he had enough money to pay for it. To a large degree this still holds true with the older generation. But the younger generation is not much different from the other nationalities. They buy on credit almost as freely as anyone else.

"The old time Finn is thoroughly honest. His word can be depended upon. In connection with our little bank we have learned this through actual experience. It is significant that during the darkest days of the depression the Finnish borrowers were able somehow to juggle along with their payments and finally to see daylight where borrowers of other nationalities would have given up and said 'Take it.' We had a number of foreclosures but only three were against Finns. The fact that the Finn dislikes to get into debt, and then only as lightly as possible, may be a factor."

The coming of winter snows brings joy to the Finns. On the day after Christmas, the celebration of Tapani calls for a sleigh ride. Moreover, during recent years in the Maple district there has been a revival of Laskiaisjuhla, or the sledding festival, a one-day celebration held in February. Various kinds of sledding vehicles, all common to the Old Country — skis, sleds, and a sliding merry-go-round — are used at a favorite spot that affords convenient slopes. For the occasion the women wear native costumes and prepare native foods. The nearest schoolhouse is turned into a cafeteria for the noonday meal, always a jolly occasion in itself. The celebrants eat heartily of fish pie, baked after the fashion of the meat pie; and lipa kaloo (lutefisk cooked with potatoes); and consume large quantities of vegetables and Finnish rye-crisp. Raw fish (silakkaa) cured in brine is nibbled with a relish common to the American who is fond of celery. Loaf sugar is enjoyed with the innumerable cups of coffee which each Finn must have daily. As with the Swedes and Norwegians, the Juhannus festival, celebrated every June 24, also is an important holiday event on the Finnish calendar.

Some who know the Finns intimately told me there is something deep in their lives that vaguely seeks articulation. They call it the spirit of romantic rhythm that centuries ago found expression in the Finnish national epic, the Kalevala. Singularly, Longfellow's "Song of Hiawatha," recounting the story of the fabled lands of Old Nokomis, whose wigwam stood on the shores of Lake Superior where the Finns have their chief settlement, portrays many characters and incidents in this Finnish classic:[75]

> *"While untilled remains the country,*
> *And uncleared remains the forest,*
> *Nor the fire has burned it over,*
> *   Vainamoinen, old and steadfast,*
> *Ground his axe-blade edge to sharpness*
> *And began to fell the forest,*
> *Toiling hard to clear the country.*
> *All the lovely trees he levelled,*
> *Sparing but a single birch-tree,*
> *That the birds might rest upon it,*
> *And from thence might call the cuckoo.*
> *   In the sky there soared an eagle,*
> *Of the birds of air the greatest,*
> *And he came and gazed around him."*

The persevering Finns have won the right to recognition as an industrious, stable and socially conscious group which any state might well be proud to assimilate for its permanent welfare.

---

[69] Langley, Thorpe M., **Geography of the Maple Area, Douglas County** Wisconsin. Unpublished thesis for the Master of Arts degree, University of Wisconsin, 1932, University Library, Madison, p. 13.

[70] Harju, Rudolph N., **Finns Pioneered Over Douglas County**, Superior Telegram, fiftieth anniversary edition, June 14, 1939, p. 26.

[71] This chapter has been critically examined by Dr. George W. Hill, associate professor of rural sociology at the University of Wisconsin, and Dr. T. A. Hippaka. professor of Industrial Education, Iowa State College; both are of Finnish descent and have written extensively on the history and activities of the Finnish people.

[72] Hawley, Zoa Grace, **Pioneers from the Northland**, Christian Science Monitor, June 29, 1938. Illustrated with pictures of Finnish customs.

[73] Central Co-operative Wholesale, in its yearbook, gives a detailed record of sales. A booklet, **Behind the Brick and Mortar**, tells the story of the Central Co-operative Wholesale.

[74] In appraising the cultural advancement of the Wisconsin Finns, the author has had the critical opinion of many residents. Valuable data were collected by Ilmar Kauppinen, treasurer of the Workers' Mutual Saving Bank, Superior.

[75] Kalevala, **The Land of Heroes**, translated from the original Finnish by W. F. Kirby. Everyman's Library, two volumes, pp. VIII-IX, see Works of Henry W. Longfellow, Vol. VI, pp. 1-197.

❖

CHAPTER XIV

Russians Bow to Eastern Cross
Clayton and Cornucopia

AN ORIENTAL, bulbous dome surmounted by a triple cross, instead of the type seen on Western churches, towered above the foliage from a rural hillside in Barron County. It was off the route of tourists' travel, and when it unexpectedly came to view silhouetted against the green of the neighboring forests its attractiveness was sharply enhanced. It appeared to be lost in this countryside of hypnotic silences, like a strange remnant of Byzantine architecture that had been sequestered on some foreign invasion. It was a Greek Catholic or Eastern church. Its members call it the Orthodox Church (the Holy Orthodox Catholic and Apostolic church) because they consider Roman Catholicism a heretical schism. Holy Trinity is one of the few Russian churches in Wisconsin.[70] Looking upon it the visitor is carried miles away as imagination crowds the mind with scenes of distant lands.

Two people — a man and a woman — were busy digging potatoes in a nearby field. To them I went for answers to my questions. And what a surprise it was! The harvesters were the pastor and his wife. Within the Russian Orthodox Church priests and deacons are usually required to wed before being ordained as clergymen. They are prohibited from marrying widows and may not themselves remarry. Bishops are forbidden marriage and are chosen from the monastic orders of which the church has many. Attending their services, I was impressed with the resemblance to the Roman Catholic rituals. Both believe in confession and priestly absolution. But there is a sharp variance on matters of faith at several vital points. The home of the archbishop for the United States and Canada is in New York.

"The three-bar Russian Orthodox cross more accurately symbolizes the crucifixion than the simple cross of the Western Christians," explained Father Nicholas Zacharkov, who paused for a talk while his wife proceeded with the potato picking.

"Christ suffered physical agony so violent that the body wrenched every nailed part out of position by thrusting one foot down and drawing the other up.

"The triple cross is the symbol of our Christian belief used on our churches, on our altars, and in our cemeteries."

The Clayton community of fifty-two families is the largest rural colonization of Russians in the state. Most of the members migrated from the vicinity of the modern Lwow (Lemberg) to Minneapolis before the turn of the century.[77] The offer of cheap lands induced their homesteading as one community in the adjoining counties of Barron and Polk.

Another group settled on the northernmost point of Wisconsin on the south shore of Lake Superior at the picturesque Siskiwitt Bay — the fishing village of Cornucopia. St. Mary's Orthodox Church was founded there in 1910 to serve the Russians who were seasonally employed in logging operations in the vicinity from 1911 to 1915. At one time this parish had a membership of over fifty, but this has since dwindled to eleven. Services are now held only on the important holidays with the priest coming from Clayton.

Because of the fewness in numbers and a lack of church facilities, most of the members of the Russian Orthodox churches in Wisconsin are now concentrated at Huron, Lublin, Kenosha and Milwaukee, the latter having three of their edifices. In 1940 there were 15,114 foreign-born Russians living in the state. Milwaukee alone has a Russian settlement of 1,500 and equally large Serbian and Ukrainian communities. The services and rites of the Russian, Greek, Ukrainian and Serbian churches are alike. The only difference among them is the language spoken.

So peaceful a secluded spot as the Clayton Russian community I have not viewed in many a day. Birds sang in the trees; the bobbing heads of children could be seen in the thicket gathering nuts; and on the crest of the valley farmers were cutting corn. As I walked across the field toward the red brick church I thought of the righteousness of the nation where people of all creeds may worship their God free from the restraints of those who may believe differently.

Within the church, my attention was first arrested by the tones of sublime colorings. Paintings offer a pageant of immortal memories. Pictures of Christ and the Virgin Mary adorn the altar, silk banners hang from standards, and Russian icons are given places of prominence. There are no pews for the worshippers. Men on the right and women on the left stand and kneel on the floor during services, facing a richly decorated altar situated on a dais one step high. No music is permitted. The attendants sing hymns unaccompanied.

Beautiful as was the interior of the church of the Holy Trinity, St. Mary's at Cornucopia inspired an even greater reverence. It is distinctive because of its enclosed altar and its ceiling studded with gold stars, rounded at the edges to give it the appearance of the heavens. Pastel shades become a prayer in these precincts. Devotion springs from the heart.

> *From Thee, great God, we spring, to*
> *Thee we tend,—*
> *Path, motive, guide, original and end.*

The Russian farmers have turned to dairying. For them there is no labor shortage. Women and children work in the fields. Their frugality has lifted the mortgages by which they made a start. They have built substantial barns and homes. With pride they send their children to high schools, where they rank well up in their classes.

A concentration of Russian laborers in Milwaukee and Kenosha recreates Old World sights even more distinctive than those found in rural life. The pictures I had built in my mind from the descriptions furnished by those who had visited these people or from the books I had read about them were quite different from the reality. The fiat of the Greek Orthodox

Church to adhere to the Julian calendar places common feasts kept with other religions usually thirteen days later.[78]

Those who follow the Gregorian calendar observe Christmas on December 25. To the children of Russia, Serbia and the Ukraine, who belong to the Greek Orthodox Church, Christmas comes on January 7. The Christmas and Easter holidays last three days, with daily church services followed by feasting with relatives and friends. The Christmas holiday has been preceded on December 6, however, by another gift event, the feast of St. Nicholas, the patron saint of Russia. Children awakening that morning find that some mysterious stranger has visited them during their slumbers to leave presents under their pillows.

For a period of forty-two days before Christmas Greek Orthodox believers have been rigidly fasting — abstaining from butter, milk and meat. On the eve before their Christmas, straw reminiscent of the stable in which Christ was born is spread on the dining room table and the frugal meal is eaten off the spread that covers it. The usual vegetables are permitted, but no meat. As with other Christians, however, their Christmas is a day of unusual festivities.

Few other religions require such long periods of fasting. Seven weeks during Lent, two weeks before the feast on June 29, for Saints Peter and Paul, two weeks before August 15, which is celebrated for the Assumption of the Virgin Mary, and the seven weeks before Christmas are the longer seasons for fasting. In addition, the Wednesday and Friday of every week come within the prohibition because Judas betrayed Christ on Wednesday and Christ was crucified on Friday. On the evening of Holy Thursday, in honor of the Last Supper, the meatless meal consists of twelve foods, mostly vegetables. One required dish is considered almost sacred. It is called Kutia and is prepared by a cooking of barley, nuts and honey flavored with poppy seed.

"And of course there is a serving of borscht," remarked the Russian priest, who had detailed for me their variations in customs with those observed by other denominations.[79]

On the Sunday before Easter Sunday, instead of blessing palms the Russian priest blesses pussywillows. On Easter Saturday at midnight Greek Orthodox people carry the cooked food for the breakfast the next morning — fancy round bread with the Russian triple cross imprinted on top, sausage, horseradish, ham, cheese and butter — to the church to be blessed. On January 20, the priest visits each communicant's home to bless it and its family.

Special days are set aside in the autumn as a thanksgiving for the harvests. On August 19, a specimen of fruit is picked from each tree in the orchard and carried before the priest. Later, on August 28, flowers of field and garden are gathered in bouquets and brought to the church. Both are offered in gratitude to be blessed. All these are seasonal expressions of nature's tribute to God.

To see the life of these people at its gayest moment one must attend a church wedding. The groom awaits the coming of his bride at a central altar in the pewless nave. She is escorted to her place at his left by the best man. Friends and relatives, still standing, close in as the priest comes in gorgeous vestments from the inner sanctuary. From then on the whole ceremony partakes of impressive symbolism. Two rings are blessed and three times received and exchanged on the fingers of the bride and groom. Crowns are placed on their heads, and holding lighted candles, they are escorted three times about the altar. Wine from the same chalice is served to them three successive times. Then, after the tying together of their right hands with a silken band the priest sings:

"Rejoice, O Isaiah. A virgin's with child and
shall bear a son Emanuel, both God and man."

Later, the accustomed mutual promises are exchanged and the crowns are removed. The whole scene partakes of the greatest solemnity. Usually more than half an hour is required for the service, with many prayers for the future happiness of the couple.

At the wedding feast which follows, their friends sing "Minohaia Lita." This is a congratulatory song accompanied by the sounds of some string and wind instruments. For no wedding celebration is complete without music.

In addition to other factors the Greek Orthodox religion finds the Ukrainians strongly in sympathy with Russia. On a boundary between two contentious nations, the history of the Ukrainians has been tempestuous, with few breathing spells of freedom.[80] Members of the Milwaukee Ukrainian community of 2,000 live in such close union that their settlement on the south side is largely an Old World colonization. Many read the Ukrainian Weekly, published in New Jersey; most of them can sing the folk songs that have been suppressed by rival powers in their own land, and on special occasions they appear in the costumes of their country.

Ukrainian women are singularly attractive in the native dress. They do exquisite embroidery work. Upon the background of unbleached linen they create in all the colors delicate patterns that are unusually beautiful. They make handkerchiefs, scarves and tablecloths, and it is doubtful if sleepers would rest well if the pillows and spread were not embroidered as custom dictates. They delight in covering with carved designs every piece of wood used in the home — chairs, tables, candle holders, platters and rolling pins.

"It is at Easter that one sees specimens of the artistic touch of our women," explained the wife of the priest of the Ukrainian Church in Milwaukee.[81] "Among friends presents are made of Easter eggs that it has taken weeks to dye and decorate."

By a process in which beeswax is used, vari-colored designs are put upon the egg with the use of a horse hair. Some patterns are reminders of the several objects of the Christian ritual — churches, belfries, chapels and monasteries. Others picture the moon, sun and stars, but the most delicate representations are of such common things as a fork, rake, window, boat, comb and powder box. It took nearly an hour for the hostess to explain to me the significant meaning of the tracery on the different Easter eggs that were displayed in a decorated basket on the parlor table.

The Ukrainians have a subtle philosophy. Their language is strewn with proverbs as suggestive of meaning as the sayings of Poor Richard. I have heard them say:

Of the evil doer — "You can tell the man by his boots."
Of the braggart — "For a time the pitcher will carry
*   water."*
Of the slicker — "Better to lose with a smart man than to
*   find with a crook."*

Wisconsin has become a haven of true freedom for these harried people from Eastern Europe, who worship their God under the emblem of the triple cross.

---

[76] This church is located in the town of Vance Creek, Barron County, three miles southeast of the village of Clayton. The first Russian church in America was built in Minneapolis in 1888.

[77] While the immigrants are Russians, they belong to a branch of the Little Russians known as Ruthenians. Ruthenians live chiefly in Galicia which before the end of World War I was part of the Austro-Hungarian Empire and which became part of the Soviet Union as a result of the German-Soviet pact of 1939. The Milwaukee Russians come largely from the Minsk region in Russia. Both speak a practically identical language.

[78] Julian calendar was that introduced by Julius Caesar in 46 B.C. The one now in general use is the Gregorian calendar, announced in 1582 A.D. and adopted by Great Britain and her colonies in 1752. The difference between the two calendars is thirteen days since 1900.

[79] Borscht is a soup made in two ways, one with meat and one without. The meatless borscht used on Holy Thursday, also called Pasmi borscht, consists of vegetables and a non-animal fat.

[80] Snowyd, D., **Spirit of Ukraine**, published in 1935 in New York by the United Ukrainian Organizations of the United States, pp. 40-48.

[81] St. Mary's Ukrainian Church, Milwaukee, is at 1231 West Scott Street; St. Sava, the Serbian Orthodox Church, is at 724 South Third, and St. Cyril and Methodus Russian Church is at 2515 South Thirtieth Street. All are Greek Orthodox.

CHAPTER XV

Voices of Little Nations
Boyceville and Willard

STANDING on the threshold of her father's home the bride had recited the customary prayer of the Slovak Lutheran faith before leaving for the church where the groom awaited.

> *My Beloved Parents: The time has now come, when I, according to God's will, must leave you. The truly good that you have done to me, and the still more pleasant life that I have enjoyed with you, makes this farewell all the more sorrowful. I know that I have received more than I deserved and that I can in no way repay you for all these many blessings.*
>
> *But I will have you forever in my memory. Although I am departing, nevertheless, I will always be your daughter, and will continue to be a decorous child. I will never forget you. For all your sincere love, for all your goodness and mercy, my dear parents, I express my cordial thanks. May God keep you in His almighty care and protection. May God graciously guide you and repay you for all the affection that you have given me. Now I commend you to my Almighty Father and wish you all His heavenly blessings. God be with you.*

It was Saturday afternoon. The farm work of the week was ended and the whole community had gathered around the little white frame edifice that hung precariously on the hillside. Weddings in the Slovak settlement north of Boyceville partake of both religious rites and civic festivities.

That same evening at 8 o'clock, the people again reassembled at the bride's home for the wedding supper. From then until midnight there were folk songs and other enjoyments. But as 12 o'clock approached the merrymaking became subdued and a tone of deep solemnity crept into the voices of the celebrants. At the appointed moment of the beginning of another day the jesting ceased entirely and the nervous bride, her long white veils streaming down her back, and her green wreath, the symbol of purity and chastity, crowning her head, took her seat where all might see. While the matron of honor removed the wreath the bride sang:

> *"Take off! Take off! Take off!*
> *My green flower wreath.*
> *Never will it, never will it be*
> *placed again on my head."*

Then a white cap, not unlike that worn by the peasants of the native land, was placed on the brow of the bride. Her days as a maiden were ended; the life of the wife was in the dawning. A moment more for the offering of good wishes and the visitors had quickly departed. Alone the young couple faced the future.

The Slovak has made respect for the parents and love within the home cornerstones in the lives of the people.

The Slovak settlement of Northwestern Dunn County, approximating 300 people, is the largest rural community of that nationality in the state. All foreign groups, however, have members among the laborers of the lake shore cities. Before coming to Wisconsin around the beginning of the century many of the first pioneers had been employed in the coal mines of Pennsylvania. But the land agent's promise of a future home of their own lured them to the cut-over country. The Dunn County colony has its own church and pastor and neighbors largely among its own people. They were truly grieved when their old country, once associated in the Republic of Czechoslovakia, fell under Hitler's yoke.

Farmers of the Dunn County Slovak settlement cure their own meats — pork and beef — using Old World recipes. Long strips of fresh meat are put into a salt brine and seasoned for a certain number of days. Then the meat suspended on poles is arranged in the roof of the smoke house and cured above a slow hickory fire. Sufficient supplies of meats are cured or canned in the fall and winter months to last through the harvest season of the following summer.

I talked to members of a threshing crew at Connersville, while the machine was undergoing minor repairs. The threshers were moving from the Slovak settlement to another community.

"We had smoked meat every day," said one of the men. "It was a great treat for us. Besides the many vegetables, they served kolace, a raised bread filled with raisins and sprinkled with poppy seed, which was very appetizing, and strudla. When at home alone these people eat several times a week of a meal made of vegetables and dumplings."

During the busy season the women work in the fields with the men. But they are strict in the observance of Sundays and holidays. Ascension is a church event of great significance in the lives of these people. In its solemn observance they read the story of their own redemption. Every fall there is a community celebration at Connersville called "Slovak Day," when many foreign garments are brought out of storage and worn. Blending with the garish costumes, the golden autumnal colors of the landscape weave a contrast of pastel harmonies. Perhaps these kindly people take on their happier moods on such occasions.

"At these celebrations we always serve the foods we like the best," interposed a mother whose family was planning the fall event. "We shall have goulash and noodles, paprika chicken, lots of vegetables, and maybe marilleinknodel for dessert."

Later I visited the Czechoslovakian (Bohemian) farmers at Viola Villa, twelve miles out of Phillips. Temptations to loiter always beset me when evidences become manifest of how these newer settlements are still storehouses of romance and representative of the types of business common to their native land. At Viola Villa I found the foreign touch deeper dyed than in the older occupied Bohemian communities around Ellisville in Kewaunee County or at Neva, north of Antigo. Five lodges in Price County belong to the Western Bohemian Fraternal Association. From time to time these groups arrange entertainment presenting Czech dances and amateur theatrical performances in which the native tongue is the spoken word. Most business is promoted cooperatively through the Czech-American National Alliance of Phillips. In religion the Czechs belong to either the Catholic or Lutheran faiths, in their churches may be heard their secular songs. But on the occasion of patriotic programs, like the anniversary of the Lidice massacre in World War II, the air becomes heavy with deep voices as they thunder the national anthem, Kde Domov Muj (Where Is My Home?). It is like the breaking of oppressive bonds when their long pent up cry through the centuries for freedom takes wing on soul-lifting words.

Baltic, Balkan and Slavic immigrants did not arrive in numbers until after 1900. Then for fifteen years the little people of Europe poured into Wisconsin and neighboring states, taking jobs in factories and mines and saving their money to buy homes. Milwaukee was to lose its distinctive German individuality to the Poles, Austrians, Scandinavians, Slavs, Italians and Greeks and to become a "Central Europe" where free men of forty-one nationalities work in harmony. Many arrived wearing the strange and brilliant garments of far-off lands; others exhibited by their personalities a suggestion of having long suffered submissively privations of the spirit. Most of them were lured to Wisconsin by the cheap lands advertised by both the railroads and the state. In forty years they had transformed ugly stretches of second-growth brush and timber into prosperous dairy communities.

World wars have taught us a new geography, have made us conscious of the vast differences politically and physically between two widely separated Slavic groups — those of Czechoslovakia and those of Yugoslavia — North Slavic and South Slavic peoples. The decadent buffer countries of Austria and Hungary held them at distances.

Serbians, Slovenes, and Croats joined on December 1, 1918, to create the Kingdom of Yugoslavia, off the Adriatic Sea, soon to be recognized by political observers as a companionless marriage. Only in blood and language are these peoples similar;

in religion and temperament the Serbs are strikingly dissimilar. Since the seventh century, when a schism split the Mediterranean world in halves, the Serbians have adhered to the Greek or Orthodox church; the Slovenes and Croats have remained Roman Catholics. The Serbs as heirs to a Byzantine civilization have kept up an incessant, age-old struggle to preserve their liberty and independence; Slovenes and Croats have been influenced through northern boundary lines for centuries by German culture. In World War II Serbians alone openly fought with the Allies; Croats joined the ranks of the Axis.

Since 1900 the Serbians have made a scattered settlement in and around Milwaukee approximating 4,500 families. They are to be found living at Butler, South Milwaukee, Wauwatosa, Silverdale, Racine, Cudahy, Mayville, Kenosha, Carrollville, and Tippecanoe. Heroism of Vidovdan, the historic day on which the Serbs met a crushing defeat at the hands of the Turks, is observed annually in Milwaukee with church services, patriotic speeches, native dances and community entertainment on the Sunday nearest June 15.

Intense patriotism marks the Serbs — love for the homeland and love for the United States. The spirit of Vidovdan pulses like a fever in their veins. History and legend have made the day the theme of hymn and epic. In 1389 the Serbs lost their national independence at Kossovo Field. The Serbian ruler, Tzar Lazar, was at that time confronted with two alternatives, either to accept the Kingdom of God, which meant to die in battle for liberty and Christianity, or to accept the earthly domain, which meant to rule his people with the help of the Turks (Mohammedans) as a vassal state. Tzar Lazar chose the Kingdom of the Spirit. As a result, his forces were ruthlessly routed by the Turks, his army slaughtered, his brave knights slain, and he himself was killed. From this heroic example there sprang the tradition among the Serbian people that it is better to die the death of a hero than to live the life of a slave. Throughout the passing centuries, this cherished ideal has faithfully been advanced and exalted.

"This concept of life has created a high sense of duty toward the country and has established the standard of 'Cojstva i junastva' (scion and heroism)," explained Rev. Milan J. Brkich, the pastor of the Serbian Orthodox Church of St. Sava. "It created national heroes not only among the educated but also among the poor and the unknown peasants. It was this same spirit that led General Draza Mihailovich and his well-known heroes, brave Chetniks, in the relentless guerilla warfare from the mountains against the Axis in World War II."

On such festive occasions as Vidovdan, the Serbians sing and dance dressed in native costumes. The ceremonies open with services at St. Sava's Serbian Orthodox Church, 724 South Third Street, Milwaukee, and usually are highlighted by the attendance of the bishop from Libertyville, Illinois, where the head of the Serbian Eastern Orthodox Church for the United States and Canada is domiciled. At such gatherings tribute is paid to a woman — Ruth Mitchell, Milwaukee, sister of America's famous General William Mitchell, the only American woman ever to become a member of the Serbian Chetnik guerillas.

St. Sava's day is observed annually in January. This occasion commemorates the services of a leader who became the first archbishop of the Serbians, the founder of their first schools and the inspiration for their cultural life.

The Slovenes are a northern nationalistic group of Yugoslavia, where their ancestors have tilled the soil since the fifth century. From Slovenia have come many of the early Roman Catholic missionaries to America, best known being Bishop Frederic Baraga, whose name and endeavors are closely associated with the development of the Lake Superior country. Their Clark County Slovene settlement around Willard embraces upwards of 200 families.

The rich ceremonials of the church are rendered even more colorful by the retention of Old World customs practiced in this Slovenian colonization. At the opening of the midnight mass at Christmas the bells are rung, at weddings "En hribcek kupil bom" and "Po Jezeru Bliz Triglava," songs reminiscent of the native land, are sung; the day before Ash Wednesday is observed with feasting and the drinking of wines, and on Holy Saturday afternoon the foods to be served at the Easter meals are carried to the church to be blessed. A small group has withdrawn from the church to establish an organization claimed to be more civic in its ideals.

There had been a family celebration at one of the Slovene homes in Willard at which I called. At the afternoon festivities Potica had been served. A portion remained and I was invited to taste of the delicacy. This is the most palatable of the many varieties of special cooking prepared for unusual occasions. It is made of a raised dough rolled out quite thin and filled with honey and nuts.

"Usually this is baked only for weddings, on Christmas day and at Easter," said the mother. "But we have been celebrating a confirmation and so we had it today."

Their harvest festival is picturesque. A dance hall is decorated with all the fruits and grains of the season. A judge chosen for the occasion presides over the events, assessing fines for offenses, true or fancied, building up a community chest that is used during the winter for charitable purposes.

Wars have wiped out many colorful customs once observed by foreign groups but have more firmly established others. Because of the world wars the poppy seed industry, indigenous of Yugoslavia, has been developed by immigrants to Wisconsin. When these blue-black seeds could scarcely be bought for use on breakfast rolls, Mrs. Steve Brajdic, of Oakfield, Fond du Lac County, started a poppy garden of less than one-half acre. Two years before the beginning of World War II the seed sold for eight cents per pound. During the war she marketed her crop at $1.00 per pound. An acre will produce upwards of 100 pounds of seed.

Occasionally some of the Slovenes from Yugoslavia will be found to have intermarried with Croatians. Their close association in religion gives them a common bond. Milwaukee has the largest urban Croatian settlement in the state and has an active Croatian woman's society which holds an annual celebration each May at the Croatian parish hall, North Seventh and West Galena Streets. The two Croatian rural settlements of less than twenty-five peasant families each are in eastern Sawyer County and at Moquah in Bayfield County, where their onion-shaped haystacks in fall attract the attention of tourists.

But the tourists may pause in wonder if their route from Northern Wisconsin takes them through Medford, in Central Wisconsin. Likely enough they will see on the streets Mennonites from their small colony of about eighty people located in the town of Holway, ten miles southwest of the city. Bushy-bearded men, wearing hats with flattish crowns and broad brims; women, their heads hidden in big bonnets, their full skirts falling to their ankles, will be seen hurrying with their shopping. They come to town riding in old-fashioned horse-drawn buggies.

"Why, these are people from another world," eagerly interposed my companion to W. H. Conrad, the editor of the local paper, when first we came upon them unexpectedly.

"Town people call them the broadhat boys because of their strange appearance," he responded, and went on to tell of their bartering for the things they purchase.

"A few pay cash for the paper but they love to trade a turkey, a chicken, eggs, maple syrup, maple cakes, sausage, firewood, any danged thing, for the paper in place of cash."

Afterwards we visited the members in their homes.[82] The Mennonites are a rather extreme sect of religious farmers. Simplicity of their ways is a noticeable austerity. The Evangelical Protestant denomination to which they belong springs from the Anabaptist movement of the sixteenth century and is so called from Menno Simons (1492-1559) of Friesland, one of their leaders. The principal tenets of the church include non-resistance, plainness of dress, rejection of oaths, adult baptism, aloofness from public affairs, restriction of marriage to members of the group and practice of the rite of foot washing.

Although the Mennonites were first attracted to Wisconsin about 1920 by the cheap prices for cut-over lands, the farming community they have developed is already in noticeable contrast with other pioneer surroundings. While they do not use tractors, their farms are well tilled. Their lands yield heavily. During the summer season the women folk make large quantities of apple butter which is sold in local stores; in the fall they manufacture a superlative bacon and sausage which have buyers beyond local confines. Fried mush and sausage make for the Mennonites their most appetizing breakfast.

The Taylor County Mennonites maintain close contact with their Dutch kinsfolk in Pennsylvania and Kansas. They belong to the Amish branch in religious belief; build no churches but meet at the home of one of the members on Sunday for morning services and the noonday meal. From their own group a bishop is selected. After marriage the male members grow a beard. Among the women quilting has developed into a fine art; seldom do they mix in neighborhood social activities. Because the Mennonite law forbids worldly images, members never have their pictures taken; because they believe too much education may lead to worldliness they discourage schooling beyond the sixth grade. County authorities have learned that the Mennonites take no interest in politics and are seldom found in trouble with the law.

These Old World customs continued in the New World have been the psychological bridge between the past and the present which made life bearable to many immigrants. Among the Hungarians of Milwaukee, the harvest festival has become an antidote for nostalgia. In 1939 Rev. Louis Balint of the First Hungarian Reformed Church found some of the members of his little flock in the doldrums to the point where, eventually, he rented a few acres of ground near Arcadia Park, had it sown to wheat, and awaited the time for nature to offer the hoped for cure of the malady. When the waving crop had begun to absorb the golden glint of the July sun, the pastor set about organizing an Old World Hungarian harvest festival.

"All our people must learn of the harvest," he announced with determination.

Officials of Milwaukee permitted an electric sign to be hung on the face of the City Hall to advertise the event. On the day

set, men and women carrying old-fashioned scythes, sickles and
rakes, led by their pastor costumed as a Hungarian nobleman
and riding a nervous horse, wended their way to the field. It was
a gorgeous array. Some of the harvesters were garbed in vari-
colored, braided vests; others had donned strange looking, white
linen trousers having the appearance of divided skirts. The
married women wore garish kerchiefs tied tightly around the
head; the unmarried girls wore a halo-like headgear called
"Parta." Somewhat awed by the pageantry of the entourage,
curious people gathered in knots to watch the progress.

No sooner was the grain laid in swaths by the sicklers than
the Hungarian women became busy. Deftly twisting select
strands into ropes, one group quickly bound the grain into
sheaves. Another group, mostly of young girls, hastily wove a
crown of the bearded heads of wheat straw, decorating it with
red and white wild flowers picked in the neighboring fields.
When the work had been finished, presentation of this bristling
emblem in the name of the harvesters was made to the farm
owner (Foldes Ur) and his wife who awaited on the veranda of
their home in much the same fashion as the Hungarian lord
receives the harvest courtesies of his obedient workers. Then the
celebrants turned to feasting, eating heartily of freshly fried
sausages, bread, and cakes all cooked and baked from Old World
recipes. Annually, but in a less ostentatious manner, on the
second Sunday in August, this Old World custom has been
repeated. Patriotic songs, Hungarian and American, feature the
occasion. It is a pretty affair that seldom fails to awaken
happiness.

The Hungarian harvest festival has become a New World cure
for homesickness and a stimulant of American patriotism.[83]

Nearly every people and creed of Europe have a pocket
colonization somewhere in Wisconsin. There is a small Lettish
settlement at Gleason, in Lincoln County, and Lithuanian
groups near Three Lakes, at Kenosha and Sheboygan.

Because of the ancient language background the Lithuanians
have interested me. I wish their Wisconsin settlements were
larger so I could study their ways and words more intensively.

No one knows what was the first language to be spoken in Europe. But H. W. Krieger, of the United States National Museum, is of the opinion that Lithuanian is one of the oldest of the Baltic branch of the Indo-European language, the parent speech of most European peoples.

The Jewish people have become prominent in the merchandising and professional life of the state, with largest numbers in Milwaukee, Madison, La Crosse and Superior. They have not formed large compact groups. In each of these communities is at least one orthodox synagogue, around which will be found what remains of Old World customs. On all high holidays the services are intoned according to orthodox ritual.

These are among the little peoples who have come to make their homes in Wisconsin as elsewhere. The story of their secluded lives is an epic in our civilization — a romance of the lives of humble men who have raised themselves to greater freedom and happiness in the face of bitter obstacles everywhere.

---

[82] **History of Wisconsin Mennonite Community,** Taylor County Star News Medford, Wisconsin, October 27, 1938.

[83] Milwaukee Sentinel, August 6, 1939 Szekely, Sari, **Wheat Fields Transplanted,** in "Eve's Stepchildren" edited by Jones, Lealon N., Caldwell Idaho, 1942, and other data furnished by Mrs. Szekely.

❖

CHAPTER XVI

Most Danish City in America
Racine

DANISH etiquette requires a resume of personal card-catalogue definiteness when making an introduction. By a single disjointed word one Dane is able to advise another of the exact status on the social register of the guest presented. It is a custom with undoubted advantages at royal gatherings, but sometimes ludicrous when tried in the mixed society of a democracy. Wisconsin saw only humor in its first attempt to introduce it on a semi-formal occasion.

"Kammerjunkerinde"— as an appended title given to Mrs. Ruth Bryan Rhode, former United States minister to Denmark, raised a flutter of curiosity in non-Danish circles when during her official service she came to Racine to speak. Anxious to meet the daughter of the "Great Commoner," William J. Bryan, women were quite baffled, however, to find the English equivalent for the long word attached to Mrs. Rhode's name as connoting some social distinction. Too proud to ask for an explanation of their Danish neighbors, they appealed for diplomatic aid in unraveling the meaning of the official honor borne by the visitor.

"Kammerjunkerinde," explained the Danish consul, "means wife of a gentleman in waiting to a king."

While that settled a distressing social problem, it also revealed the Danish custom of preceding the man's name by his title or occupation and extending it with an added "inde" for his wife's.

"Sometimes these title handles create funny situations," volunteered a Danish woman. "Hans Christian Andersen, the writer of fables, has poked fun at some of the linguistic monstrosities which in this way may occur, as, for instance, when he tells about 'Gedebukkebens' (Billy goat bones), 'Overogundergeneral' (over and under general), and 'Kommandersergeant' (commanding sergeant). Still, when you receive so much information right away about a person to whom you are introduced it gives you some idea of his background and social standing."

Danish traditions are strongly rooted in Racine. For more than half a century it has been known as "the most Danish city in America." Of the 40,000 Danes in Wisconsin a majority live in Racine County, an estimated 18,000 in the city alone. The past lies in wait to greet the visitor in all sections. So much kringle, a common item in the diet, is sold in the bakeries of their neighborhood at the western outskirts that their settlement has been popularized by the name "Kringleville."

Danish settlers began coming to Racine and Kenosha as early as 1843, the year of the outbreak of the first Schleswig-Holstein War. But it was not until the late sixties and the seventies that the real invasion set in. Then every boat brought immigrants. The Mitchell Wagon Works and the J. I. Case Company drew them in numbers. For years the Mitchell Company employed Danes almost exclusively. By 1920 there were more foreign-born Danes in Racine than groups of any other nationality. Even the Scots, whose unusual January celebration of the anniversary of the poet Robert Burns had long been an event of social importance in Racine, were to find their voices almost drowned out.

Moreover, all through the latter half of the nineteenth century a steady procession from Denmark was in progress. These little groups were scattered over the state, to grow within fifty years into distinctive Danish American settlements at Denmark, Brown County; Oregon and Brooklyn, Dane County; Poysippi, Waushara County; Neenah, Winnebago County; Ashippun, Dodge County; Big Flats, Adams County; Suring, Oconto County; Rosholt, Portage County; West Denmark, near Luck, Polk County; Washington Island, Door County. One of the largest rural Danish settlements in Wisconsin is in and around Waupaca, and one of the most compact centers is about Withee in Clark County. There is no county in the state that doesn't have a few Danish American citizens. Next to Racine, the largest urban group, nearly 3,000, are settled in Kenosha. Most of these city dwellers work in factories.[84]

"Many came to win an economic freedom which seemed impossible under the existing conditions in old Denmark," Rev. Jens Christian Kyaer offered in explanation. "Not all came with the understanding that they would stay for life, but most of them who came to Wisconsin remained."

Several of the settlements have established community gathering places. At Racine the Dania Society and the Danish Brotherhood have built imposing modern club houses — the one to serve social groups for the cultivation of music, literature, debating and the languages, and the other for popular entertainment, home talent dramatics, and the furnishing of fraternal insurance. Within both clubs the business sessions and the official records are in Danish; both have libraries of over 3,000 volumes in Danish; both continue as centers of Danish community life — gathering places for dancing, wedding anniversaries, singing societies, and the playing of schervinsel. Abelskiver and coffee are always ready to be served. For many years the Danish Hall at Waupaca was a live center of Danish culture and activity, housing a library of over 2,000 Danish books. The Danish church and community hall in Withee are still an active center for a Danish life and culture of a very high order. The strong family organization of rural Denmark is to be seen in the great-family or kinship groupings (family reunions) held every year in Wisconsin Danish settlements. As many as fifty and sixty relations groups meet in Waupaca County yearly to celebrate family festivals.

The Withee community has kept alive one Old World custom that carries with it a dash of both sentiment and affection. When any couple has a golden wedding the church congregation gathers at evening in the Danish Hall where the tables are especially decorated for festivities. An appropriate program is arranged, speeches are given, and lunch is served. Afterwards the couple is presented with a gift from the church. There is much group singing at all such events.

Home gatherings are not as a rule invitational affairs. It is an open house for all. When anyone has a birthday all friends gather to help celebrate. The minister and his family arrive early. The usual coffee is served; cards or games of that type are not played, but singing and conversation are the entertainment. Danish birthdays are festive occasions. In many homes the "abelskive" pan is brought out, because all comers love sausage. The social spirit that arises from such evenings becomes the bond which knits a strong community fabric.

The Danes are a cheerful people. They welcome visitors with a hasty "God Dag." As a general rule they take their entertainment seriously. They are not satisfied to be amused; they want to learn something at the same time. Annually, the first Sunday in August is dedicated to a Danish American basket picnic in Racine, attended by delegations from every section of the state. I went along to mingle in crowds whose songs and laughter also made me happy although I could not understand. Processions marched to the grounds bearing the United States and Danish flags. Speakers extolled the courage of Danish people and reviewed their achievements in this country. Bands played Danish airs. The Danish Sisterhood glee clubs sang native songs. A holiday spirit ruled completely. The soul of old Denmark lifted the hearts of the celebrants to visions of deathless glory.

Christmas is the Danes' most important home event. Like their Old Country neighbors, the Swedes, they participate for two weeks in celebrations and festivities. From our Lord's birthday until Epiphany their social life alternates from fireside to church and back again.

Since 1928 a Sunday-hour radio program, consisting of classical and semi-classical Danish music, has been conducted from a Racine station. It has often been said by tourists from Denmark that the presentation is enjoyed more than programs offered in Denmark. A showing of Danish-made films is an almost weekly event at clubs and movie houses; several home talent plays in the Danish language and with Danish costumes are annually presented to popular audiences. When the Crown Prince and Princess of Denmark came to Racine for a visit in 1939, more than 30,000 Danes took over Racine, and a newspaper columnist, unable to get a place in the receiving line, dryly observed:

"So with flying flags giving Racine a holiday atmosphere, there's something special about this day, with the visiting Prince and Princess from Denmark."

But Crown Prince Frederick saw in the countryside, where they had settled, scenes that reminded him of Denmark.

"The rich farmland, the dairy cattle and cozy farm houses recall to our minds the Danish Islands," he observed in addressing his wandering people. "I feel this is particularly true of Wisconsin. The Dane who left his home shores for a wider horizon and new lands has found them amid familiar surroundings." [85]

The reputation of the Danes for truth telling is proverbial. Two Danish ministers in Racine, arrested for speeding, were brought before Peder Back, the creator of the first all-Danish radio program in this country, who held the office of justice of the peace.

"Are you guilty?" Back demanded. Each parson protested innocence.

"Cases dismissed," announced the official. "A greater judge than I shall judge you."

On my many tours to the Wisconsin Danish-settled communities, representative citizens have gone with me wherever I desired. Out in the farming district of Waupaca County I visited a Danish pioneer who, with young and old, was commemorating Denmark's "Grundlovsday," the peaceful granting of a free constitution to the Danish people in 1849. At Withee, a Danish farmer exhibited his hobby of carving small, beautiful wooden chests after a Danish folk pattern centuries old. During times of leisure I visited their homes, their clubs, the factories where they work and the churches they attend. The

Danes of Wisconsin are lovers of good books, flower gardens and pictures just as were their ancestors back in old Denmark. The Danish family is an enduring institution. That is a distinction worth more than material progress. With them emphasis is placed on "human values and relationships, things not so easily seen and observed." [86] All the impressions may be summed up in a single observation: the common understanding of these people has kept alive the prevenient spirit of comradeship with the Old World while deepening a patriotic love for the United States. It is hard in a democracy to abandon the customs that have taken centuries to acquire. But the innate desire of liberty seems to have been always in their hearts awaiting only the propitious moment to give it expression. Wisconsin offered that opportunity.

Scattered throughout Racine and Kenosha are Danish Lutheran churches, restaurants and stores. Racine has eight Danish bakeries. Wherever I went, I saw typical Danish beauties, fair haired and blue eyed, stalwart prototypes of ancient Vikings.

Danish clubs and restaurants have the Danish smorebrod, similar to the Norwegian smorgasbord, where as many as fifty cold dishes are offered. At Sunday dinners the Danes are fond of a fowl stuffed with prunes and apples, instead of dressing, and roasted, dumplings, red cabbage, pickles, beets, potatoes, kringle or pumpernickel bread, with a dessert of apple cake covered with whipped cream. For lunches and for a midnight snack they demand open-faced sandwiches spread with rullepolse — medister pole. Taverns serve the famous Danish akvavit, distilled from potatoes, flavored with anise, malort, popularly called "wormwood" by the occasional drinker, and Kirsebaer liqueur, a cordial made from cherries.

When times are normal the Wisconsin Danes keep in close touch with friends in the homeland. Occasionally the King of Denmark will send a cablegram of greeting in recognition of some local celebration. Twice special royal honors have been conferred on immigrants. When Hitler invaded Denmark, Racine went into mourning, and the Danish flag was flown at half-mast from the Danish community buildings.

"Denmark's sorrows and joys are ours," sadly observed a Danish cobbler from whom I sought information. I felt that these people have a community sense of responsibility — the kind that each individual owes to a neighbor.

Something homespun in Danish character is evidenced in the domestic life. Danes are a people of small, comfortable homes.

"I dislike to be away for an evening meal," apologized a Danish farmer to whom I had extended an invitation to dine at a restaurant. "Danish wives make it a practice to serve Danish cooked foods at night. And then — there are the children."

Few authors have ever been able to interpret children as has Hans Christian Andersen, the famous writer of fairy tales. If there are any pupils in Racine who do not know that Andersen was a Dane, their teachers could not name them. Visiting presentations of "The Ugly Duckling" or the poor little match girl who died, a waif in the cold night, dreaming of a grandmother who welcomed her to paradise, draw capacity crowds. Danish people talk of these inimitable character episodes as though they were family traditions. Their children have come to feel at home in this land of fantasy.

Perhaps the greatest contributions made by the Danes to their new homeland are practical lessons taught in cooperative organization, in marketing and in the modernization of agricultural education. Both ideas are of Old World parentage. The Danish system of cooperative management has been generally adopted in Wisconsin. The application of the Danish "folk school" idea to agricultural education taught at the University of Wisconsin has given a new vision for the rural outlook.

A study of agricultural development in Wisconsin convinced the dean of the Wisconsin College of Agriculture, Chris L. Christensen, himself of Danish blood, that one of the new business trends will be a wider spread of cooperatives. Before coming to Wisconsin in 1931, Dean Christensen spent years in Denmark observing the farmer-owned cooperative system in operation. Today Wisconsin is a leading cooperative state. The Danes, Norwegians, Swedes and Finns have done much to make it so.[87] One of the few tobacco associations in the United States to survive the erratic market is the Northern Wisconsin Tobacco Pool which operates in Norwegian settlements. In 1940 seven hundred farmer members of this cooperative marketed more than three million pounds of Type 55 cigar leaf tobacco having a total value of one-half million dollars. The regular growth in membership in this organization is indicative of the excellent results secured in favorable prices to the growers.

The major part of the Wisconsin cranberry crop is marketed cooperatively through the Wisconsin Cranberry Sales Company, an affiliate of the American Cranberry Growers' Exchange of New York. Sales of this fruit crop reached a value of $900,000 in 1940. The Wisconsin association has operated continuously since 1906.

The Fruit Growers' Union Cooperative, located in the Door County peninsula, was reorganized in 1933 with 600 members, and its total volume of business in the sale of fruits and the purchases of supplies exceeded one-half million dollars in 1939.

Another splendid cooperative enterprise among farmers in Wisconsin is the Cooperative Wool Growers' Association which marketed in 1939 over a half million pounds of wool and pelts for an income of $200,000.

Fifty-five percent of the entire state production of butter is produced in cooperative creameries and the output totals over 100,000,000 pounds annually. At 1943 price levels, the value of this output would approximate $50,000,000. Two creamery districts and several large plants as well as the Wisconsin Cheese Producers' Cooperative market their products through the Land O' Lakes Creameries, Incorporated, the largest cooperative butter and cheese sales organization in the United States.

The Badger State produces one-half the national production of cheese, three-fourths of which is of the cheddar type called American cheese and one-fourth classified as foreign types. The total production exceeds 407,000,000 pounds. Practically all the cheese production in Wisconsin is organized on a cooperative basis in approximately 1,900 factories, although an appreciable percentage of the factory properties is owned by the cheesemakers. The business of manufacturing cheese involves pooling and cooperatively sharing the expenses and the proceeds from the production. Wisconsin Cheese Producers' Cooperative is a federated sales organization of 65 cheese factories with headquarters at Plymouth, and with six other assembly locations. Sales of cheese, dairy products and other supplies will, at present prices, probably run close to $2,000,000.

There are approximately 200 cooperative livestock shipping associations operating in Wisconsin, 80 percent of which ship at least a part of their supplies through terminal livestock sales associations in the central markets.

The most notable of these terminal associations operating in and near Wisconsin are The Equity Livestock Sales Association, of Milwaukee, The Central Cooperative Commission Association of St. Paul, The Chicago Producers' Commission Association, and The Farmers' Union Livestock Commission of St. Paul and Chicago. Sales of livestock through the Equity Livestock Sales Association of Milwaukee were over $8,500,000 in 1939.

There are about 240,000 policyholders in Wisconsin who carry their insurance on farm properties in 200 mutual companies with a total insurance in force of well over one billion dollars. In addition, there are 13 farm mutual windstorm insurance companies which insure Wisconsin properties for a sum of 400 million dollars. This type of mutual enterprise has been in continuous operation in Wisconsin since 1860 and provides an invaluable service at greatly reduced costs. The Danish cooperative influence, so widespread in Northern European countries, has been the agency for infusing a greater business stability into Wisconsin undertakings.

"Recognizing that cooperatives have become an advancing factor in the solution of agricultural problems, the University of Wisconsin College of Agriculture founded a school for the training of cooperative managers and directors," reported Dean Christensen. "Ten years of this service-training has turned the old pathway strewn with wrecked cooperatives into a business road paved by sound financial experience bearing big dividends to farm markets."

Then there's the revised Farm Short Course at the university, one of the great forward steps in American education. It was started in 1932 on a pattern of the Danish "folk school."[88] It aims to train farm boys for rural leadership as well as skilled farmers. Academic requirements for entrance are tossed to the wind. Students may not even be high school graduates but they must have at least two years' experience on a farm and a determination to return and stay on the farm. It is a two-year, fifteen-week farm short course of the non-credit type of education with no degrees. Less than $100 a year will pay the entire educational outlay.

"The course of study is organized around the idea that these young men are going to be farmers, citizens and community leaders at one and the same time," Dean Christensen explained. "We have, therefore, completely blended the so-called vocational emphasis with the scientific, cultural and citizenship emphasis. For example, there are courses in music, drama, citizenship, history, law, speech, and public discussion scheduled right through the day and interspersed with courses in livestock management, soils, field crops, feeds and feeding. There are courses with scientific and fundamental content such as nutritional chemistry, bacteriology, genetics, economics and sociology.

"We believe that an individual is not a farmer one day and a citizen the next. Therefore, we are trying to observe unifying educational principles which will help these young men to think of all the phases of society, to consider their own lives as a whole, and to regard their citizenship as an everyday affair."

Farm students hear lectures in the agricultural sciences and cultural subjects. On three or four evenings each week they participate in forum discussions. Businessmen and dirt farmers who have made good are enlisted as special speakers at these "evening forums." It's just the sort of a practical education that a wise farmer hopes to leave to his son as an inheritance. It's one of those pioneering experiments that Wisconsin always engages in when there are prospects that the people may get a new vision on life. Ten years is a short time in which to measure a movement, but the results are already apparent in the spread of modern agricultural methods throughout the state.

This practical turn of Danish thought, stimulating a man to help himself by his own initiative and through cooperation, may become a vital contribution to the building of a new ideal of social leadership.

---

[84] Lind, William, Racine, Wis., has compiled a series of scrapbooks on Danish activities in Wisconsin, which have been the source drawn on by the author in writing this chapter.

[85] Address, Crown Prince Frederick, Memorial Hall, Racine, April 24, 1939.

[86] Christensen, Chris L., address before the Danish Brotherhood at Racine, January 10. 1942.

[87] For story of the extent of the Finnish store co-operatives around Superior, see Chapter XII, supra.

[88] For Dr. Glenn Frank's own story of his dream of the Danish Folk School Farm course and of its inauguration under Dean Chris L. Christensen, consult Proceedings of the University of Michigan for 1937, pp. 471 -473.

❖

CHAPTER XVII

Sarsa Time and Spaghetti
Madison and Milwaukee

IT is sarsa time in Madison. The hot August sun has ripened the tomatoes, and Monona Bay that skirts "Little Italy" seems congealed in silver silence. It is the season before the gnat invasion.

All along lower Regent Street, in adjoining back yards and open spaces off Milton Street, Italian housewives are vigilantly guarding the sarsa boards from the threat of rain. Within the homes the kettles are boiling — big kettles filled with sliced red tomatoes. When after an hour the cooking has turned the bubbling pulp into a thin sauce, the contents are strained. Then the squashy mass is poured on clean white sarsa boards and placed in the sun to evaporate. Every hour, or oftener, the thickening nucleus is spread and respread until it takes on a richer shade and becomes a heavy relish. As it is packed away in jars, olive oil is poured on top — enough to form an air-proof covering. The finished product is then ready for use — all fall, all winter, all spring — until another crop of red tomatoes can be harvested.

"How do you use it?" I inquired. "Does it take the place of butter?"

"Oh! No! It is put in gravy, or added to peas, stew, egg plant, macaroni or spaghetti. It is a relish that makes either meats or foods more palatable. Everybody in Italy makes sarsa."

More than all that! More than a seasoning it surely must be. I have a feeling that restaurants where Italian spaghetti is served would not be so popular without sarsa. Spaghetti and sarsa are family favorites for Sunday dinners. Both are staple products in groceries wherever Italians make their home.

The motive for the coming of the Italians was not born of religious or political oppression like the earlier waves of immigration from North Europe that swept into Wisconsin. Rather the impulse prompting the colonizations half a century later from South Europe was economic. Crowded conditions account for the influx. The first ten years of the century registered the largest numbers. Now the native-born Italians and their descendants in the state exceed 32,000. By 1900, less than a dozen had arrived to make their homes in Madison. The number has since been multiplied more than one hundred times. A similar influx occurred at Hurley, Kenosha, and Waukesha. Each urban settlement offers as many varieties of dialect as there are provinces in Italy — Lombardian, Sicilian, Albanian, and Ambruscian.

Genoa, in Vernon County, is the Italian hill town of Wisconsin. It is a miniature of the famous Genoa at the foot of the Alps, which gave Christopher Columbus to America. Stone buildings bear the architecture of houses to be found in Italy, the village road that follows the foothills is set with business places displaying Italian names. Picturesque reels of the fisher folk, who brought their ancient vocation with them, make colorful an old Mississippi River "slough," now known as Genoa Bay. Views up and down the valley give one a sense of isolation and peace. On the upper route of the Mississippi River it is doubtful if drowsy Genoa can be excelled for sheer Old World attractiveness.

Two rural Wisconsin communities settled by Italians have become distinctive for specialized agricultural pursuits. Members of the Barron County group near Cumberland came as railroad strike-breakers but remained to farm. They have helped to make the humble rutabaga worthy of a fall festival with a reigning queen. The Marinette County colonization at Pound has given impetus to the manufacture of a special quality of Italian cheese that stimulates hunger and makes spaghetti dishes a rare delicacy.

There is something uncanny about the way events shape themselves to reassert the old adage that history repeats itself. Fond du Lac County, which claims the first cheese factory in the state, founded at Ladoga in 1864, became, three quarters of a century later, the center of the nation's Italian cheese industry. Wars in Europe account in large part for the decline in foreign imports and for the miraculous increase in the Wisconsin production. The record in 1939 was nearly equal to the total United States imports of cheese from Italy during 1940. Dairy plants in Fond du Lac County made 3,866,000 pounds of the 1940 Italian cheese, thirty-one percent of the state's total production; Dodge County ranked second with twenty-one percent, and Polk County third with twenty percent of the total.

Even Wisconsin's famous dairyland displays foreign nationalistic traits. So many varieties of cheese are made that instructors in the Dairy School at the State University are able to predict in part the nationality of a locality by the methods of cheese manufacture as described by students. Less than a dozen concerns are engaged in producing the five principal Italian types. They include the Stella Cheese Corporation, Campbellsport, with factories in eight other communities; Tolibia Cheese Company, Fond du Lac; Belmont Cheese Company, Mayville; S & R Cheese Company, and S. Pasini, both at Plymouth; and Frigo Brothers, Pound. Maps on the factory walls show the bootlike land of Italy and the Indian face of Wisconsin — now market rivals.

"At present the industry serves a sectional market," explained a factory manager. "The Italian cheese industry is still in its infancy. Some day leaders hope to inaugurate an educational campaign to sell the public on the edible, nutritious value of the product. Much the same processes are employed in the making as when Caesar's Roman legions were rationed on cheese centuries ago."

Italian cheeses vary in size from the shape of a bread loaf to a toy balloon blown up to look like a torpedo, and in weight from one pound to an eighth of a ton. Often the cheese curing room resembles a gymnasium overcrowded with punching bags. Provalone, used for table purposes, has a sharp and aromatic taste; Asiago has a sweet flavor and is flavored for grating; Parmesan appears in bread loaf form and is generally served with spaghetti and other Italian dishes; Ricotta is utilized in the making of candy, and Gorgonzola is a blue cheese employed as a savor for soups. The principal Italian cheese markets are found in the eastern states.

"It is the zip of Italian cheeses used in most Italian cooking that has popularized spaghetti dishes especially with the American public," explained the chef of a Milwaukee restaurant. "No single Italian custom has been more universally adopted than the eating of spaghetti. Our trade is more American than Italian."

Restaurants and stores offering spaghetti are not confined to the Italian districts. So Americanized has the dish become that it is served regularly by hotels and boarding houses. A ready-to-eat canned meal is sold by city grocers generally. The trade in the unprepared product in Italian settlements is in the staple class with meat and vegetables.

The business sections of Italian colonizations are a curious blending of the old and the picturesque with all that is new and businesslike. On the same street with fine stores that cater to metropolitan trade are little hole-in-the-wall places where a few vegetables, cans of tomato paste and bottles of olive oil give evidence of a shopkeeper. The show window of a Madison grocery was piled high with bundles of green roots when I strolled through the district.

"What is this you are selling?" I asked.

"It's anise root," the clerk replied and waited.

"But how is it used?" I parried, not knowing whether it was a fruit or a vegetable.

"It is served and eaten the same as celery hearts. It is more delicious and aromatic."

When my order was wrapped, my attention was attracted to a corner of the store that appeared like a pioneer apothecary shop. Large cans and glass jars were filled with dried plants.

"These are the herbs and seeds used by the Italian people in the making and flavoring of their many varieties of soups and stews," the clerk volunteered. "These jars contain anise seed, chili peppers, sesame seed, rose marine, bay leaves, lentils and oregano. The herb oregano is imported from Greece and is more savory than sage."

On the floor beneath the shelves were wooden pails partly filled with navy beans, lima beans, kidney beans, chick peas and rice. On the lower shelves were containers of olive oil. There was a low consultation between the clerk and the proprietor as I stood around reading labels on packages. From my interest they knew I had other questions to ask.

"In season artichokes are a favorite," said the clerk as I took down a fruit jar. "For use out of season we sell them preserved in olive oil. All classes of Italian people are as fond of these native foods as are those other nationalities who prefer sauerkraut or potatoes as staples in their diet."

No one who came to trade seemed in a hurry. Customers paused in the aisles to greet each other and visit. They listened with keen interest when mention was made of their native land. Customarily the women wore a scarf about the head. Their conversation was in dialect. Leaving, I visited also the little homes of the people — many of them ill-kept in outward appearances. The scene was one of children playing in the cramped yards, gourd vines trailing on back fences, knots of men gathered on the street corners to chat, dropping their voices as I passed.

Italian workers have shouldered the manual burden of railroad and sewer construction performed by the Irish immigrant a century ago. They are small of stature but contractors have found their physical endurance phenomenal. Wherever possible they join the trades — bakers, barbers, musicians, cobblers, scissors-grinders, marble cutters and peddlers of fruits. The Italian women design beautiful artificial flowers, which they sell from door to door in communities beyond the settlement.

For the Italian, classical music seems a natural inheritance. Many opera singers who have appeared in Madison and Milwaukee are Italian by birth — Nino Martini, Tito Schipa, Ezio Pinza. Their concerts are liberally attended by the low-wage earners in the settlement. Often the man who digs sewer ditches or works as a street scavenger will be found in the front row to be jostled by the elite in formal dress. Ethereal ballads carry them to heights of ecstasy.

Italians are fond of processions. Columbus Day, on October 12, is celebrated by them with the noise and fireworks of an old-time American Fourth of July. They like to march in parades carrying the American and Italian banners at the head of a column. Church "fiestas" offer a chance to dress up. At least one such brilliant affair is staged annually at the Madonna De Pompeii Church in Milwaukee, the largest Italian Roman Catholic congregation in the state. On that occasion the dingy neighborhood takes on life and color as the men, garbed in native costume and marching in fours, carry on their shoulders around the roped-off streets statues of St. Joseph or the Virgin Mary. A crowded line of enthusiastic, devout parishioners follows. Booths line the walks where foreign cooked foods are sold; giant firecrackers explode to rock the neighborhood; snatches of native songs fill the air; there is a blare of Italian music; the gladness of greeting translates diverse dialects.

"Little Italy" plans and waits for months the coming of this fiesta time. Racine, Kenosha, and Madison hold similar celebrations, less august because of their smaller colonizations. Smoothly dressed youths mingling with men and women attired in garish Old World clothes weave a fascinating human pattern obliterating lines that mark the hemispheres. I was loath to leave these simple, charming people who today had momentarily turned back the clock of the centuries to live in fancy with the apostles and martyrs, to breathe the air of olive groves and to glimpse the blue peaks of the Apennines.

Within the Italian homes special church rites touching family occurrences are celebrated in an extravagant way. After the baptism of a baby, which is generally delayed until ample funds have been accumulated for a feast, relatives and friends are invited for a jubilation. The whole Sunday is given to the festivities. Italian foods are served; homemade wine is drunk — both often in excess. There is music, and noise stirs the community, so much that neighbors sometimes are known to complain of the din. To help defray the expense participants pin dollar bills on the white garments of the sleeping child.

Special events occurring in adult life have deepened my impressions. Months before a wedding the parents of the bride visit all friends to extend a personal invitation to a shower. The men who come are served beer and an alcoholic drink; the women are given wine. Trays of home-baked "dutchi" take the place of pretzels or crackers. Soon everybody is trying to get in a word. All sit around as each gift is unwrapped and admired. Later when the wedding takes place, a dinner is served at a community hall where as many as 300 may sit down to eat a meal cooked from many an Italian recipe. The feast is concluded with serving of roasted almonds and chestnuts. During the afternoon, while the guests look on, only the members of the wedding party dance. This is considered a concession so all may have the opportunity to see the swish of elaborately formed dresses and witness an exhibition of dancing as a fine art. In the evening, all participate in the dancing and the festivities.

A death in an Italian home may take on a weird aspect. The wife or mother will sit by the dead for hours chanting a self-composed wail that relates in broken sentences and pitched notes the history, deeds and virtues of the departed. Except that a member of the family leads the recital, this dirge resembles the keening of professional Irish mourners or the Jewish lamentations over their dead — the latter customs no longer observed in this country. Sometimes at the grave the bemoaning recital will be renewed. If the family can afford it, the tombstone later will bear a conspicuous portrait of the deceased embedded in the face of the monument by a weather-resisting porcelain process. Thereafter the widow will wear the mourning black for years.

The custom of lighting candles on the graves of the dead on the night before All Souls' Day is still widely observed in Wisconsin Catholic communities where people from Italy, Germany and France are settled. It is a custom so old that the origin is lost. As night approaches on November 1, relatives and friends gather in the cemeteries. Altar boys light the candles while the watchers pray for their departed. At Calvary in Milwaukee, Holy Cross in Madison, and St. Mary's in Burlington, the recollections are almost as universally kept as is Memorial Day in the spring.

"We have heard that the custom came originally from Italy,"

Father Edward J. Kersting, Burlington, remarked. On the morning following the candle services, special masses for the dead are held in all Catholic parishes.

"Little Italy" holds its own fashion parade every Sunday. Members of the younger set find in attendance at mass an opportunity to display their new clothes. Girls exhibit a fondness for the brighter colors; the older boys are clean shaven, their clothes pressed, their hair slicked, their whole attire and appearance of the latest fashion. Customs require that fathers who still have handlebar mustaches wear them waxed, curled and turned up at the ends.

There seems to be a universal opinion among social workers and others who have close contact with the Italians that the home lacks discipline. It is the mother's duty to manage affairs. But she spares the rod and children are allowed to do much as they please.

"We give them the sweet life, while they are young," declared an Italian mother.

The father brings his money home and turns it over to his wife. He insists, however, that he be allowed to do the Saturday shopping for foods. He will work hard all week, but Sunday he is prone to overeat. Italian wives watch the bargain advertisements in the papers and often will appear at the store two hours before opening to be on hand for the best selections.

The coming of the Italians to the urban centers of Wisconsin has resulted in a kaleidoscopic shifting and reforming of the older settled districts. More than 12,000 Italian Americans now make their homes in Milwaukee. The Third Ward, once the bulwark of the Irish, has succumbed to the invasion; the German district of Madison has been affected also by their crowding. Troubles in Europe are erasing the mark of their stolidity; the public school is grounding them in the ways of a democracy. Deep down in their hearts these people are proud to be American citizens.

❖

CHAPTER XVIII

Poles Rejoice in New Freedom
Milwaukee and Polonia

S T. JOSAPHAT'S green dome dominates the skyline of the South Side in the city of Milwaukee. Toward afternoon friendly shadows melt the surrounding little homes of the Polish people into its extended wings. A foreign visitor who looked upon it for the first time called it the Chartres of America. The renowned artist, Frederick Polley, who came to sketch it and give it a place in his series on America's grand buildings exclaimed in admiration that he had found it "something so beyond the commonplace that it borders on a real thrill."

Southsiders call it, more in love than in accuracy, the "Polish Cathedral." Its imposing grandeur makes their hearts beat with pride when they contemplate its ageless permanency. It has real nobility. Built in the form of a Latin cross, it is one of five basilicas in the United States.[89] Populations may shift and churches be moved to accommodate changing conditions. But a basilica never. Its altars and stations, always carved from marble, become a part of the consecrated earth from which the edifice rises. Six granite columns are a pedestal for a heroic statue of the martyred Polish saint of the seventeenth century, whose name St. Josaphat's bears. Its jade dome — 204 feet high and 80 feet in diameter — is comparable with St. Peter's; its beautiful rose window and Raggi's paintings are art treasures worthy of special recognition.

How St. Josaphat's came to be is a story bred of the fortitude and piety of immigrant peoples who fled Russian oppression to make their home in Milwaukee. Their pastor, the Rev. William

Grutza, called "the blacksmith priest," was dreaming of a new church to be erected of brick and mortar when he read in the paper that the old Chicago post office building was to be razed and sold.

"I need that," he exclaimed, and went out to raise the money to build a grand church for his exiled peoples. But the cost of transportation and rebuilding exceeded so many times the wildest estimates, that the parish debt rose to $300,000 before the building was finished in 1898. Broken in health, the dreamer returned from a rest sanitarium and said the first mass but was unable to remain for the dedication in 1901. Through all the following years of financial distress, the expatriated Poles remained steadfast. Ultimately it became necessary for the Milwaukee Archdiocese to share a part of the heavy burden. Finally, in 1929, Pope Pius XI, who in earlier life had served as an apostolic delegate to their homeland, raised their edifice to a basilica. The dream of the blacksmith priest had come true — realized at last — although he had long since gone to his reward. St. Josaphat's envisions the life and the history of the Poles of Milwaukee — church and home.

The Poles are now the second largest nationalistic group in Wisconsin, exceeded only by the Germans. The Norwegians are third. The tragic consequences of the Polish insurrection against Russia in 1863; discriminating legislation by Russia, Austria and Germany limiting political and economic rights and religious privileges; difficulties in obtaining land to work and opportunities to obtain cheap acres in America — all operated to send a tide of immigrants to Wisconsin following our Civil War.[90] The characteristic pattern included previous years of stinted savings while employed in skilled or semi-skilled labor. After one in Texas, the next earliest settlement in the United States was made at Polonia in Portage County in 1857. Despite the barrenness of the sandy soil, the infiltration numbers increased rapidly, mainly from the peasant class. The Poles have prospered as farmers where others might well have failed.

Out in the open country they erected in 1934, at a cost of $75,000, one of the largest rural churches in Wisconsin north of

Milwaukee, rivaling, if not exceeding, in beauty the edifices at Pulaski and Independence. It has a seating capacity of 1,200. All sermons are preached in the Polish language. From stained glass windows on opposite sides of the nave, two Polish saints, Casimir and Hedwig, look down with admonishing eyes upon the worshippers.

"I always have capacity attendance," said Rev. Leo Jankowski, the pastor. "Neither rain nor cold, neither morning nor night will deter the parishioners coming to announced services. Portage County alone has eight Polish congregations."

Confines of their settlement in Portage County and in other Polish colonizations are marked by wayside crucifixes set up at rural crossroads.[91]

Since 1866, when the first Polish church was organized in Milwaukee, the urban Polish population also has steadily multiplied. Seemingly Poles make good in both rural and city surroundings. It is estimated that their numbers, including descendants, now exceed 300,000 in Wisconsin; foreign-born in 1940 were 31,487. Important groups are found also in the cities and communities of Beaver Dam, Berlin, Bevent, Galloway, Green Bay, Hatley, Independence, La Crosse, Manitowoc, Marinette, Menasha, Pulaski, Stevens Point, Superior, and Thorp.

About one-half the farm population of Portage County is Poles; over 100,000 Polish residents live in Milwaukee County, requiring one Polish orphanage, sixteen Roman Catholic churches, one Polish National Church and one Polish Baptist Church to serve their religious needs. Milwaukee also boasts of a Polish high school and over eighty societies that serve their charitable, religious, economic and patriotic interests. "Sokols" are organized for physical exercise. Within business fields there are several Polish building and loan associations.

Stevens Point is probably the most characteristic Polish city in Wisconsin. Rural settlements round about make it the hub of their activities. Citizens think Polish. A professor who had never before visited Stevens Point made this inquiry at the hotel desk:

"What is the population of this city?"

"Polish," was the response of the clerk as he turned to other duties, believing he had given a complete answer.

The public square in Stevens Point is an interesting place on market days, especially on Thursdays and Saturdays in winter time. Almost anything grown or made on the farm is put on sale — butter, buttermilk, cottage cheese, dressed poultry, Polish sausage, hogs, beef, eggs, hay, cattle, cordwood and many other products one would not surmise are produced in the region.[92] The color of the scene has special charm for the stranger.

In rural and urban life the Poles are markedly different from their neighbors. They live comfortably and prefer neat and clean garments to expensive and gaudy apparel.

"People will not remark on what you eat, but they can see what you wear, and according to that they will judge you," is a quaint observation often repeated to me when among the Poles.

Their families are large — sometimes of ten or twelve children. One instance of twenty-two children, all at home, was brought to my attention. Millet's farm paintings showing whole families working in the fields are realistic summer spectacles in Polish country districts. It is a current aphorism that they live off the produce that cannot be sold. Outsiders have jestingly named their colonization of several towns around Stevens Point the "Kerosene County." Milwaukee's South Side Polish section is also a scene of contrasts. It is characterized by few apartment buildings — rather by little individualistic homes, a garden and a patch of lawn.[93] But whether they live on the farm or in the city, the Polish are hard working, family folk, clannish to a degree that they become a nation of themselves.

Centuries that have passed and countries that are far away color the everyday lives of these people. There is probably no other nationality that clings so tenaciously to its language. The youngsters are taught to learn and love their mother tongue and to read Poland's brave history.

When the grotesque hat craze of the second World War epoch caught the fancy of American women, Polish wives and daughters quite generally clung to the simpler headgear, many retaining a scarf or kerchief tied tightly under the chin. The scarf has meandered back into style. Intermarriage between the Poles and other nationalities is rather uncommon. Also men who change their surnames for an easier pronunciation are frowned upon by the rest of their countrymen. This nationalistic feeling among the Poles is fostered by the numerous language papers — political, religious and cultural. Within recent years, however, the Poles have been entering into politics. Judge John C. Kleczka of Milwaukee was the first Polish congressman from Wisconsin. The right to vote is the leavening force that makes us all one.

The Poles rejoice in their new freedom. During the first World War the number of Polish volunteers was out of proportion to the Polish population. Moreover, since 1874, Poles have been active in the Wisconsin National Guard, and the South Side Armory — called Kosciuszko Hall by older Poles — continues as a rendezvous for Polish American patriots in Milwaukee. Never do the Poles forget the patriots of their native land. Two Milwaukee parks bear the names of their heroes — Pulaski and Kosciuszko. There are several Wisconsin communities with Polish designations: Sobieski, Krakow, Pulaski, Casimir, Poniatowski, Lublin, and others.

The Poles are successful farmers. They possess a capacity for drudgery. Potato growing has become a symbol of agricultural attainment. It is a family industry, in which women wield a shovel with the best diggers in the patch. Every farm home has an ample basement in which a part of the surplus is stored to await favorable marketing conditions. Besides, there are numerous commercial warehouses in the sand belt where the crop may be sold at harvest time. However, competition of other states has discouraged many Polish farmers. There are indications that the potato belt may be forced to yield to the invasion of dairyland.[94]

Within smaller communities, where lands are available, the Poles turn to gardening, raising good crops of potatoes and vegetables. Their Italian neighbors do the same but the contrast in articles produced is noticeable to even a casual observer like myself. Both work their land well. But where the Polish gardener plants mostly root crops—potatoes, rutabagas, turnips, beets, and possibly peas and beans, the Italians prefer lettuce, endive, lima beans, peppers and tomatoes. Root crops are always predominant in Polish gardens.

There is nothing of the social climber instinct in the Poles. Younger men hire out to work on neighboring farms; girls seek domestic and factory employment in cities, but the city bred have an increasing tendency to enter business and professional life.

But whether they work on a farm or in the shop the Polish love of music is evident. There are singing societies for the young and the old, for women and for men, and finally mixed and single choirs. Preferred are the melodies that lend the magic of old to the deeds of their patriots. Polish bands and orchestras are found in many of their settlements.

Church holidays and festivals of all sorts are numerous. These people enjoy dancing, and wedding celebrations partake of the nature of a three-day marathon, preceded by the removal of the veil and the crowning of the bride. Then with every man in the community awaiting his turn to "break the plate" with a silver dollar offering and have his swing with the bride, the social occasion is eventful. The custom is for the man who dances with the bride to smash a cheap plate with a silver dollar, and if he does not succeed in the first attempt this sum forfeits to the bride and he must keep on spending until successful. This rite is slowly changing because of the high cost of living, jobless years, and the scarcity of the silver dollar. But there is no substitute for dancing. That is a social inheritance as cherished as is the family name. Weeks are spent in baking and preparation of foods for weddings. Exhaustion of the principals usually ends the celebration.

"Polish sausage, sauerkraut and potatoes!" There was a pause after each word and a smile on the lips of the Portage County farmer as the articles were enumerated. "These foods make Christmas for me."

Out in the woodshed he showed me a rack from which sausage rings, suspended in air, already were seasoning. And this was six weeks before the holidays.

Several times throughout the year the high school Polish clubs of Milwaukee present free performances of music, singing and dancing. Costumed dolls illustrating distinct and social types of dress in Poland are displayed. The Mazur Polish Dance Circle stages the varying wedding ceremonies common in the native land; such Old World customs as Szopka, Jaselka, Kulig, Swieconka, Sobotka, and Wianki, and such dances popular among young people as the Comic Devil, the Naughty Naughty, and the Walosz, a Silesian waltz. A five-hour continuous program is sometimes necessary to satisfy the large crowds which come. So typical of Poland are these festivities that the Milwaukee group has given exhibitions in all Polish-settled communities in Wisconsin and made one appearance on a folklore program at Washington.

"Milwaukee Poles still observe many Old World customs in their homes," explained Alfred J. Sokolnicki, the instructor for the Mazur Polish Dance Circle. "Among others, on Shrove Tuesday, the day preceding Ash Wednesday, the Poles celebrate the last day of parties and festivals by baking and serving 'pontshki' (doughnuts). This practice signifies that during Lent meat will be forbidden, except on certain days. At midnight all social activities cease until Easter Sunday. This festival compares with the Mardi Gras.

"Then with Easter Monday comes the 'Dingus' or 'Smigus' (switching day). Wearing the strange costumes of Poland, boys call on their favorite girl friends and switch them with perfumes or douse them with water. This custom is said to have begun in the days of Christ. When our Lord had risen, the inquisitive people gathered around His grave but would not leave at the command of the guards. When switches were used unavailingly, then water was tried to finally disperse the crowd. On Easter Tuesday the girls have the opportunity to avenge the previous day's activity. They, too, have a switching day and make use of it to switch the boys."

Of more significance in Southern Wisconsin is the pilgrimage to the St. Francis Monastery and College of the Franciscan Fathers at Burlington, on the first Sunday in August. To this annual event come several thousand worshippers from other states. It is held only in Franciscan churches. As many as a score of choirs participate. Religious ceremonies, the singing of ancient hymns, and marching in colorful procession mark the occasion. During the day the traditional observance of this Feast of Portiuncula, suppressed in Poland during the Nazi regime, is re-enacted on a scale as it was in Poland before 1939. The patriotic hymn sung by the army of the immortal king, John III Sobieski, when it turned back the threatened Moslem invasion at Vienna, is played by the bands to rally the visitors to a rededication to old ideas. Religion and patriotism fuse to make this occasion eventful.

"The Polish American parish is not a mere copy of the old Polish parish, but a combination of parish, village and commune," concluded George W. Hill, associate professor of rural sociology at the University of Wisconsin, after a four-year survey in which census reports were studied and hundreds of persons interviewed. "Customs change but the things which do not change are the ideals and values with which we look on life. They stay with us. Scratch the surface, generations later, and you will find those values."

To the Poles, life is a cycle often made beautiful by biblical pageantry. To them, as to several other nationalities, the story of the Three Wise Men of the East who came from far away to offer their gifts at the manger-cradle in Bethlehem partakes of present-day reality. Occasionally in the Krakow parish, north of Green Bay, and now and then in other communities, the old Polish custom for boys to dress up as the Magi is revived to emphasize the majesty of the Epiphany. Garbed in gaudy costumes — one dressed as an Ethiopian — and accompanied by the priest, they wend from house to house and farm to farm singing Christmas carols. Then the priest blesses the home and marks the door with chalk. The older Poles, who remembered this observance across the Atlantic, await with joyous anticipation the coming of these visitors. It is as if they, too, in their wanderings had seen the star in its rising and had followed it into the free democracy of Wisconsin. And their journeys, like that of the Magi, ended by tendering their gifts of loyalty to new masters.

[89] Basilicas in the United States are located in Minneapolis, Minn., Lackawanna, N. Y., Milwaukee Wis., Baltimore, Md., and Conception, Mo. For detailed story of St. Josaphat's, see Stoer, Frances, **Cathedral of Milwaukee's Poles**, Milwaukee Journal, March 10, 1940.

[90] Snyder, Helen Marion, **The Foreign Population of Wisconsin**, thesis for Ph.B. degree, University of Wisconsin, 1920; Tomkiewicz, J. W. S., **Polanders in Wisconsin**, Proceedings of Wisconsin State Historical Society, 1901, pp. 148-152; Sanford, Albert Hart, Polish People in Portage County Proceedings, supra, 1907, p. 259.

[91] Two distinctive wayside shrines are to be found, one about one mile north of Pulaski on the road to Krakow (Wis. 32), and a second a short distance east of Sobieski on Oconto County Trunk Line S.

[92] The Very Rev. Stephan Dzialdowski, 0. Praem., Green Bay, who has served as a priest in nearly a dozen Polish parishes of Wisconsin, has furnished me with many of the facts and incidents presented in this chapter.

[93] Kerstein, Edward, **Polish Pioneers**, in Milwaukee Journal, February 9, 1941.

[94] Hill, George W., and Smith, Ronald A., **Men in the Cut-Over**, Research Bulletin, 139 April 1941 Agricultural Experiment Station, University of Wisconsin, p. 49

❖

EPILOGUE

WISCONSIN is distinctive as a state because a blending of Old World population with the Yankee stock has resulted in founding a successful agriculture, has culminated in diffusing education among the masses, and has flowered in an awakened citizenship that makes the Wisconsin way the touchstone of democracy. The ripening fruit is not from the tree of any one nationality. It is a hybrid.

Wisconsin began its career as a Yankee state. The severe lines of their lean-to homes, the occasional, still standing landmarks in octagon houses, the more prosperous pioneer builders of which had adopted the Orison Fowler Hudson Valley fad of the early fifties — these mark the limits of their early invasion into Southern Wisconsin. Within a half-century, however, their numerical importance was threatened by the coming of three-quarters of a million people from across the ocean who were stirred by visions of a better life. These were the most restless, ambitious, adventurous members of stable, Old World societies. Vitality and determination flowed in their veins. They came to win — to build for themselves. The grand audacity of a wild, untamed frontier rose to challenge them, but they had no fear. They knew that to reach the peak of high attainment man must sweat and toil. And by their hardships they achieved. Even at high tide the total of all foreign-born was less than 37 percent of the population. By 1940 the ratio had declined to about 9 percent in a total population of 3,139,587. Until the turn of the century, eastern states furnished three-fourths of the governors, Germany one and Scotland two. The shrewdness of the Yankee had a primitive grip on the state that is still felt.

The prairie section of South Central Wisconsin became known to the newcomers as "Yankeeland"; a compactness of German settlements along the lake shore and wooded areas brought the appellation "Teuton State." Often Dane County was extolled as a "Norwegian principality." A fusion of efforts and the Americanization of all these foreign groups behind the leadership of the Yankee gave impetus and character to the state's high accomplishments.

As with their social customs, indigenous to these Old World peoples, so their recreations are perpetuated in the love of skiing by the Norwegians and Swedes, of curling and golf by the Scotch, of specialized gymnastics by the Germans, and of boxing, football and horse-training by the Irish.

Credit for popularizing improved livestock must go to the Yankee.[96] But it was the patience and care given by the German, Norwegian and other foreign groups to the breeding and raising of farm animals that have given strength and position to the industry.

Credit for leadership in developing dairying also must go to the Yankee. But again it was the frugality and attention to the undertaking of the foreign-adopted elements that have made dairy farming an outstanding success. And when the Yankee grew restless it was his Old World neighbor who bought his acres and went on with the endeavor.

Credit for inspiring the establishment of a common school system and kindergarten instruction must go to the Germans, but it was the Yankee who impressed an advanced tone on the state's policies of higher education. Small colleges founded by Yankees in South Central Wisconsin became beacon lights for guidance. The sons and daughters of the foreign-born quickly caught the visions of a broader life and incorporated them into their everyday living.

When it came to reforms in government, however, it was the influences from the aroused Old World sections — Germans, Irish, Norwegians with others — that recruited the ranks. They made possible the triumph of the movement for "a genuinely, democratic, popular government";[96] they gave to public life a moral tone that no racial substitutions can obliterate.

Wisconsin is the soul of a great people. She manifests the

spirit of the conqueror, whose strength has subdued the forest, quickened the soil, harnessed the forces of nature and multiplied production. From her abundance she serves food to the world.

"I have come to expect the impossible of Wisconsin," voiced an astonished World War I general after he discerned the loyalty of her men and women at home and the bravery of her sons on the battlefield. Racial admixture has spiritualized the state's destiny, her daring and her distinction.

Wisconsin life is like the fabric that comes from a vast loom, firm and strong — all wool and a yard wide. Daily the workers weave a story in patterns. Sometimes the yardage is plaited with fantastic figures, emblematic of a joyous life, sometimes its smooth surface records chapters of heroic deeds; always it voices a rhythm of contentment. It is the chant of united, happy peoples — of badgers all.

The fabricated epic reveals the dreams of the pioneers that have come true. Here, where they have found "the art of living joyfully and dying with a fairer hope," the grandeur of their accomplishments has bloomed into a common heritage, fit to endure.

---

[95] Schafer, Joseph, **Yankee and Teuton in Wisconsin,** Wisconsin Magazine of History, Vol. VI, p. 277; **Wisconsin's Changing Population,** Bulletin of the University of Wisconsin, Serial No. 2624, October, 1942, p. 11.

[96] Roosevelt, Theodore, Introduction to **The Wisconsin Idea,** by Charles McCarthy, New York, 1912.

❖